Typographical
Ornaments

Typographical Ornaments

Philipp Luidl
Helmut Huber

Blandford Press
Poole · Dorset

First published in the U. K. in 1985 by
Blandford Press Ltd., Link House,
West Street, Poole, Dorset BH15 1LL

Distributed in the United States by
Sterling Publishing Co., Inc.,
2 Park Avenue, New York, N.Y. 10016

British Library Cataloguing in Publication Data

Luidl, Phillip
  Typographical ornaments.
  1. Printers' ornaments
  I. Title   II. Huber, Helmut
  686.2'24   Z250.3

ISBN 0 7137 1641 X

Originally published in 1983 as
Ornamente-Ornaments by novum press
World copyright © Verlag F. Bruckmann KG,
Munich, Germany.

English translation by Lenore Lengefeld.

Designed and produced by F. Bruckmann KG.
Printed and bound in the Federal Republic of Germany.

Contents

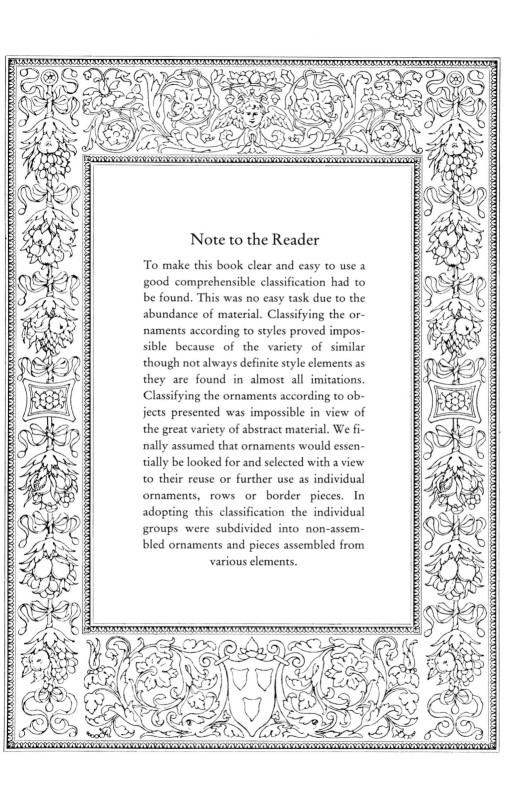

Note to the Reader

To make this book clear and easy to use a good comprehensible classification had to be found. This was no easy task due to the abundance of material. Classifying the ornaments according to styles proved impossible because of the variety of similar though not always definite style elements as they are found in almost all imitations. Classifying the ornaments according to objects presented was impossible in view of the great variety of abstract material. We finally assumed that ornaments would essentially be looked for and selected with a view to their reuse or further use as individual ornaments, rows or border pieces. In adopting this classification the individual groups were subdivided into non-assembled ornaments and pieces assembled from various elements.

M.

Attempt at a definition

"Ornare" is Latin and means "to adorn". It would offer a too-simple solution, however, if we were to stop at this statement. For a hat or a plume may be an adornment; yet neither of these may be an ornament. The hat, at least, is meant as a protection from heat, cold or rain, while the sole function of the ornament is to decorate something.

In order to define the limits of this concept more easily, let us compare the ornament with another element of form: the symbol. The symbol is an emblem; the ornament is not. The symbol has an exactly defined form; the ornament does not. The number of forms or subjects present in the symbol is precisely determined; in the ornament it is not. The symbol is provided with a chosen color; the ornament is not.

When a symbol is observed by different persons, they all recognize or acknowledge the same meaning in its form. This can lead to a situation where, as in the raising of a flag, they even react in unison. The ornament communicates no agreement, nor does it serve as the message of any cult. Its only purpose is to adorn.

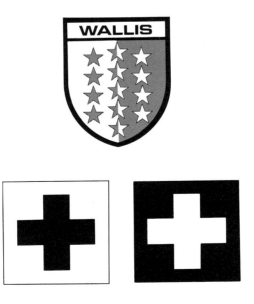

The symbol stipulates, as in the case of the Valais escutcheon, that thirteen five-pointed stars must be displayed, since these represent the thirteen early Christian communities of the Valais. The star as adornment does not refer to any specific number.

Let us take another example, also from Switzerland: the simple symbol of the country itself – the cross. The color of this cross is vital, inasmuch as the same cross in a different color would become a completely different sign. The ornament may be depicted in any color.

While the symbol, as we have proven, always communicates a certain meaning, the ornament is in contrast completely free of significance. It can only be judged on the basis of its aesthetic value. Yet if the ornament represents a form devoid of significance, this does not mean that it must be a non-representational form. The ornament may consist of representational, as well as non-representational motifs. The object illustrated has simply lost any relation to its original meaning.

On the origin of the ornament

Symbol and ornament are not always clearly distinguishable, above all in their earliest manifestations, when it is likely that the ornament evolved out of the symbol. It is not historically provable, although easy to imagine that water and oil jugs, for example, were marked with distinguishing symbols. Let us assume that water was represented with a wavy line and oil with an olive, that is, with a circle or an oval. It was soon discovered that both symbols could serve not only as designations on the jugs, but also as decoration. Water and oil symbols were woven together, resulting in a wreath, and its inventors were delighted with the successful symbiosis. And since this improved the jug's attractiveness and value, the "decoration" was applied to other objects as well, without carrying over the original meaning. The symbol became an ornament.

At another point in history, people wanted protection from "evil powers". They were given symbols as magical signs, a sort of amulet or talisman. Much later, when the meaning of these signs had been lost, they were still worn as adornments and souvenirs.

If, in our first example, we have shown the translation of linear and geometrical forms in symbols into the same kind of forms in ornaments, we may infer that our second examples originated in plant and animal motifs. Both examples are only hypotheses. But the few scientific findings in this area are not contradictory. The third conclusion, however, is based on scientific fact: that an ornament motif points to its place of origin. It is true that the oldest forms of the ornament, such as wavy lines, zigzags or spirals have been found among many different peoples. Yet the meander must be of oriental origin, since the river which it represents is in Asia Minor. Most ornaments which depict animals were inspired by species indigenous to Persia. The acanthus is of proven Grecian origin. Arabesque and Mauresque are designations for ornamental forms which clearly stem from the Arabic.

The solid ornament

Here we are primarily concerned with architectural additions and the embellishment of necklaces and bracelets. The decoration may be raised or engraved, similar to the fluting of columns, or it may be free-standing, as seen in Gothic windows. While master builders constructed ornaments from stone, plaster and wood, goldsmiths worked with precious metals and gems, shells or bone.

Not every material, of course, is easily workable. And so representational motifs were simplified because of this problem. Abstract forms were often developed whose original designs were not planned as such. Materials and tools pointed these forms in a direction which might never have been taken under other circumstances. Successful design is often predicated on man's ability to recognize and accept the peculiarities of his materials and tools.

Solid ornaments have often served as inspiration for printers, who seldom resisted the temptation to simulate a three-dimensional effect. This weakness may be observed up to the present day. Although the architectural element in printed ornaments is no longer clearly recognizable, their simulated depth leads us to the conclusion that this is actually the case.

Mauresque with scrollwork. Peter Flötner, about 1546

The pictorial ornament

Fresco plaster or canvas presented a material and the brush a tool which were much easier to manipulate than those used in the creation of solid ornaments. Nevertheless, it is amazing to see how often the brush is wielded to imitate solid forms. There are many examples of illusionistic ornaments in the history of art, above all from the Renaissance. Certainly the specific painting technique employed – fresco, oils, watercolor or tempera – exerted a strong influence on the results achieved. Yet these techniques did not mold the form of the ornament as strongly as did wood or stone. In contrast to contemporary architecture, which is distinctively free of ornamentation, modern painting has incorporated the ornament as an essential part of the composition. This does not mean that it appears only in the frame or border of a picture, as in earlier periods, but that it may actually influence the pictorial content. Here works by Willi Baumeister, Paul Klee, Georges Braque and Henri Matisse come to mind.

By reducing its variety of colors and nuances to a single hue, the art of printing has incorporated the pictorial ornament while often borrowing its simulated perspective.

The woven ornament

Among all the tools used to create ornamentation, the loom is without doubt one of the most suitable and historically perhaps the most significant. Today the woven ornament has been supplanted to a great extent by the printed ornament. However, much of the wealth of printed ornaments of the past has been adapted for contemporary textile designs.

The printed ornament

The invention of the printing press was doubly significant for the development of the ornament. Firstly, it was absorbed into this new technology, which meant that new forms would of necessity be developed with these new tools. Secondly, ornaments could be collected and thematically classified, to be sold as specimen books. This was an important step in the propagation of the ornament; today these books serve the art historian as research material. Forms and styles could be copied much more quickly and easily. The ornament was no longer confined to space or time.

The invention of the printing press is generally conceded to have taken place in 1450. At that time, at least in German-speaking countries, the Gothic style dominated. The first printed works were executed in Gothic lettering, while book decoration was still handpainted by illuminators. Only the text was printed; however, initials, pictorial elements, foliage and tendrils were painted on. Printed decoration is seldom seen in Gothic works. Beginning with the Ren-

End-pieces with tendril decorations, 17th cn.

aissance, this phenomenon was encountered more and more frequently.

The printed ornament must also be precisely classified; on the one hand, symbols must be excluded, and on the other, pictorial representations obviously intended as illustrations. The concept, "printed ornament", means a decoration which may be repeated, which has no other effect than to lighten the surface of a page or sheet or to frame it, to direct the reader's eye here or there. The ornament can divide as well as unite, yet it can never deliver a message or an interpretation.

In the course of our analyses, we will very likely venture into border territories where it will be difficult to differentiate. However, we would like to try to follow our criteria as closely as possible.

Guilloched border, middle of 19th cn. ▷

C. E. WEBER

SCHRIFTGIESSEREI, STUTTGART

Gegründet 1827

1827

1827

EINFASSUNGEN FÜR
WERTPAPIERE

The tool as formative instrument

The fact that the traces of the tool can be seen in the decoration is easily proven: the original Sumerian/Babylonian characters, probably executed with a reed or chisel, change to cuneiform lettering when inscribed onto clay with a bone stylus. The completely different appearance of Asiatic lettering as compared with that of European countries may be attributed to some extent to the fact that in China, Japan or Korea, writing was executed with a pointed brush, while in Rome a slanted quill or flat brush was used for writing and to trace letters.

Both of these techniques employ the brush as tool, but each in a different way. Another element exerts an influence not possible to the same degree with other tools: the varying way the brush or quill is held. Since, for instance, the Japanese write not only from top to bottom, but also from right to left, and with a very fluid ink, the brush must be held at an acute angle so that the still-wet characters will not be smeared. They write, as it were, from the top down, while the Romans hold their brushes diagonally and write in a way similar to our own.

An example of a tool which markedly characterizes the object it creates can be found in the woven ornament, which together with the painted ornament served as model for the printed ornament.

Since the printed ornament was always produced by means of a printing form, with tools which varied greatly while still conforming to the specific printing technique employed, we have chosen to classify these ornaments according to the processes in which they were printed.

Letterpress printing

The German terms, *Buchdruck* and *Hochdruck,* refer to the same process: letterpress printing. Requirements for this process are a printing form, printer's ink, a printing press and the material to be printed, usually paper. The printing form must fulfill two conditions: it must be mirror-inverted, and the matter to be printed must be raised above the surface; in other words, it must be a relief. There are several methods for producing such a relief.

16

For the *woodcut*, pear, alder, cherry or nut wood is usually employed. If the wood block is cut longitudinally from the tree trunk so that the grain runs in parallel lines, it is called a long-grain woodcut. If the plank is cross-cut, so that the age rings may be seen, it is called a cross-grain woodcut. The tools employed may be knives, single lip cutters, chisels and gouges or the V-gouge. Even in works of great artistry, it is apparent that not only the carver's tool but also the wood itself contributes to the effect achieved. Woodcuts were first created as illustrations at the start of the fifteenth century, and have held their position as an artistic technique up to the present day.

The *white-line cut* may be compared to a photographic negative. The resulting picture receives reverse-tone values, but is otherwise produced like the woodcut.

The *dotted print* is executed on soft metal. The main tool used in this technique is the center punch, since the motif is created in a manner similar to pointillism. This technique is particularly suitable for the creation of ornaments.

The *wood engraving* is executed on a boxwood end-grain block. With the single lip cutter, or scorper, not only fine lines but also dots are cut. In this way varying density of the lines and dots allows the build-up of a kind of screen, on which many degrees of tonal shading may be achieved. Wood engraving was renamed xylography in the 19th century, when it came into popular use for illustrations.

The *linocut* is created from linoleum or plastic material. The areas *not* to be printed are incised with knife, scorper or rasp. Although very similar to the woodcut, the linocut does not achieve its purity of line or fine surface texture.

Gravure printing

The techniques of gravure printing are similar to those of letterpress printing to the extent that in both processes a relief is employed. In gravure printing, however, the areas to be printed are not raised but recessed in the form. First the printing is completely covered with ink, which is then removed from the surface with a doctor blade, leaving ink in the recessed areas. This ink is then printed onto absorbent paper under pressure. The deeper the recessed areas, the more ink is retained, which results in darker tones.

Copperplate engraving, as its name implies, is the execution of engraving on copper plates. A single lip cutter is used to engrave lines in the plate. Here, as in gravure printing, the motif must be mirror-inverted. The cutting of these lines demands great strength. The severe physical discipline of this art is also reflected in the appearance of the finished work. When the burr, or rough edge created by the etching is removed, the plate is then blackened. The ink is polished off with a cloth and finally with the ball of the thumb. The ink remaining after this process is printed onto paper. Copperplate engraving was invented about 1420, and retained its popularity well into the 19th century.

The *scratchboard technique,* or *Mezzotint,* is also executed on a copper plate, which is roughened with a special tool called a rocker, or cradle. Its rocking motion creates an over-all burr of projecting points and edges. The areas to be white in the print are painstakingly rubbed with a burnisher and an engraver's scraper. The ink remains only in the roughened areas and is wiped away on the smooth ones. Intensity of tone can be regulated by the degree of surface roughening, which results in very fine tonal shadings. While other techniques employ fine lines to create a picture, in Mezzotint engravings the entire surface of the plate is treated. This technique was invented in 1642 and is still in use today.

The *drypoint technique* employs a metal plate upon which a mirror-inverted motif is inscribed with a steel needle. The fine ragged edge or burr resulting is retained, since it takes up additional ink, and the surface is cleaned. This process lends the finished print a darker tone. The drypoint technique, or drypoint engraving, was invented in 1480 and is still popular.

The *etching* is also created by means of a metal plate, which is covered with an etching ground (wax, varnish or asphalt). The mirror-inverted motif is etched with a needle onto this ground, exposing areas of the metal plate. Now the plate is washed with a mordant; only the

Renaissance vignette, Italy

bared lines are affected and thus deepened. The etching ground is then cleaned from the plate and it is blackened. After the surface is polished again with cloths and the ball of the thumb and is free of ink, the print is made. The first etching was printed about 1513. Almost no other graphic technique is employed as often by artists today as the etching.

The *aquatint* is similar to the mezzotint in its treatment of the plate surface. While in the mezzotint this is accomplished by mechanical means with the roughening tool, the aquatint is created by etching with a mordant. Asphalt, resin or colophonium dust is melted onto a copper plate. These dust particles create a screen upon which a series of fine pits are etched, that is, around each minute spot of the acid-resistant dust. The fineness of this screen is determined by the size and density of the dust grains. The biting process is often executed over an etching; in this case the aquatint is simply a background etching. This technique was invented about 1768, and is still in use today.

Planography

Planography is actually a separating process. The mirror-inverted motif is drawn with a grease stick, a crayon or an inked pen onto a fat-free stone plate (limestone shale). The stone is then covered with a solution consisting of gum arabic and thin nitric acid. In this way the free areas of the drawing become water-soluble. This means that the stone plate is divided into fat- and water-bearing areas. It is then moistened and blackened with fatty ink. The areas which have absorbed the water now repel the ink, and vice-versa.

Lithography, or *stone lithography*, can be distinguished from offset lithography in that the print is made directly from the plate, while in offset it is made not from a stone but a metal plate, which is transferred onto a rubber impression sheet and then onto paper. Since offset is a transfer printing process, the artist can execute his drawing true-to-side on the plate. In 1798 Aloys Senefelder invented stone lithography, a process which today is still in the forefront of graphic art.

Screen printing

Screen printing or *serigraphy* are the names best known for this art of printing. In these processes, a taut mesh is employed, which may be made of steel, gauze, nylon or other materials. Its sole purpose is to serve as the base for a stencil. The stencil may be cut from paper and applied to the mesh or it may be sprayed or painted on to stop out the nonprinting areas. The ink is spread over the mesh with a squeegee; in this way it penetrates the mesh over the free areas of the stencil and is carried onto the paper or other printing material. The invention of screen printing is dated at the turn of the century, yet it would appear that its real discovery as an artistic technique is now taking place.

Title page of "The works of Geoffrey Chaucer" ▷
by William Morris, Kelmscott Press 1896

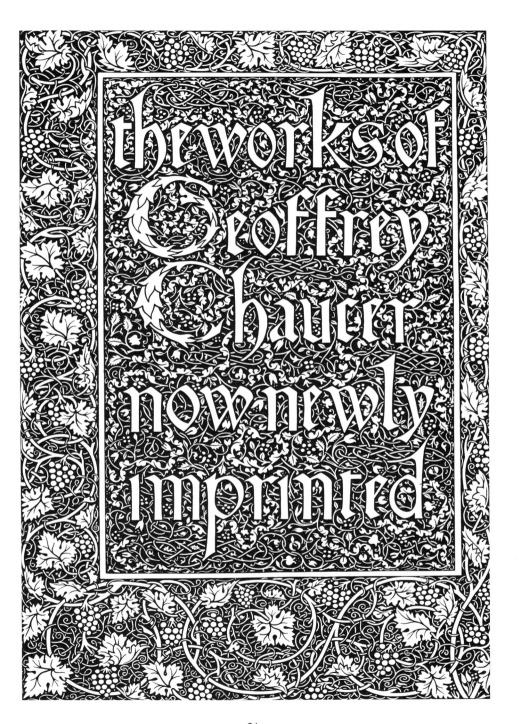

the works of Geoffrey Chaucer now newly imprinted

The historical period
as formative element

An influence even stronger than that of the tool was the period in which an ornamental form was created. Each era has its own fashions, which gradually solidify into a characteristic style. The origin of this style can be traced to a definitive social structure, and may be recognized not only in clothing but also in architecture, sculpture, painting, poetry and music. Since ornaments may be classified as falling between architecture and painting, like these arts they are also subject to the influences of their period and its styles.

The Gothic period (1150 – ca. 1500)

This is the era which saw the invention of the printing press, and so we will begin here with our stylistic analysis of the ornament. Architectural forms provided the chief inspiration for the Gothic ornament, which is why its motifs consist of the trefoil, quatrefoil, sixlobe tracery and paisley. More seldom found but none the less important is the interlace pattern, which resembles twisted or plaited bands. Plant motifs yield the richest treasure of designs. Almost every leaf and flower form is to be found, from the grapevine to maple and oak, ivy, ferns, broom, hawthorn, snapdragon, juniper and water lily.
The spare, ascending lines of the early Gothic period become even longer and thinner in late Gothic works. Leaf motifs display an increasing abstraction. Animal motifs from Roman times are still used, but gradually lose their symbolical content. Beasts are slowly transmuted into fabulous creatures.

The Renaissance (1500 – ca. 1600)

Although like every other art manifestation the ornament also has its roots in antiquity, for some time to come the Gothic period still holds sway. Renaissance ornaments are characterized by their symmetry. The hop and fig leaf are added to already existing plant motifs. Another novelty is a composition made up of weapons and music instruments, which takes its place in the history of ornamentation as the "trophy". Animals are stripped of their natural appearance and remodelled into griffons and other fabulous creatures.

The main embellishments of the early Renaissance (1520–1570) are grotesque, mauresque and basketwork. In the high and late Renaissance period (1570–1620), scrollwork and strapwork dominated.

Grotesque is a symmetrical ornament. On both sides of a vase or jug form, leaves and fabulous creatures are entwined.

Mauresque displays no representational motifs. Since the Islamic religion forbids the depiction of humans or animals, Moorish decoration is made up of combinations of lines and forms. In the 15th century, mauresque wandered from Byzantium to Rome. In Germany it was only popular as a model for textile patterns up to the middle of the 16th century. Dating from this period are the example or specimen books which exerted such a strong influence on the German Renaissance ornament.

Basketwork is related to mauresque to the extent that it is also said to stem from the Orient. Lines and bands are plaited or woven into curious figures which are usually of geometrical design. Basketwork is a pure line motif without any additional elements.

Scrollwork is actually a border ornament. It bears a resemblance to rolled thongs, snails or the volutes of Ionic colums. The cartouche is the diminutive form of this kind of border.

Strapwork takes as its model the wrought-iron fixture. While scrollwork appears three-dimensional, strapwork seems flat, although this does not prevent it from successfully simulating the fixture with its nails and bolts.

The Baroque period (1600 – ca. 1730)

This classification stems from the Italian language and stands for the ornate, the exaggerated. Baroque brings the dissolution of regularity of form; the motif receives sweeping curves and corners are avoided. New form elements include the shell and the putto. Out of scrollwork and strapwork are created the auricle or volute style, which

commands the scene from 1580 for almost a century. Then the acanthus motif becomes popular once again. In the high or late Baroque period from about 1680–1715, the joy of inventing forms rises to a delirium. Straight lines are barely tolerated and every curve is carried to extremes. Preference for curlicues goes so far that it includes lettering, making an ornament out of the monogram and allowing the symbolic content of the letter to drown in decoration.

The Rococo period (1720 – ca. 1780)

The name of this period derives from the French word, "rocaille", and means shellwork. And the shell is truly the basic motif of the rococo style, although its form is bent asymmetrically to take the shape of a "C". This also occurs in the volute. Trophy motifs include musical instruments, rosebuds and bands. Ornamentation now becomes light and flame-shaped; it is almost at the point of dissolution. If the ornament, up to now, was an embellishment, the rococo period makes it the main objective. This goes so far that the form of objects is secondary to the decoration. Toward the end of this period, Asiatic patterns appear which, however, survive primarily as decor for furniture, textiles or porcelain.

Neoclassicism (1770 – ca. 1830)

Again and again in the history of art, we come across a kind of nostalgic movement. If the previous style was carried to extreme lengths, the following is sure to fall into its formal antithesis. The vertical exaggerations of Gothic are broken by the horizontal planes of the Renaissance. The exuberant forms of rococo are followed by the sobriety of classicism. Very often a past style and its form elements experience a revival, and this may likely be one that lies several epochs in the past. Thus the Renaissance paid homage to Roman antiquity, the Baroque period borrowed elements of the Gothic, and Neoclassicism is derived from styles of antiquity. Classical ornaments such as the meander and the running dog are revived. Cartouches become oval, urns and garlands become the main motifs of classical ornamentation.

The *Empire* style is a variation of neoclassicism which is better described as the Napoleonic style. Decorations include the laurel, lotus, sphinxes and pyramids, all decorations referring to Napoleon's Egyptian campaign.

Romanticism and *Biedermeier* may also be categorized as outshoots of classicism; these styles create an aura of domestic tranquillity. *Neoclassicism* or *Hellenism* also fall under the definition of classicist ornamentation, since they are too derivative to be considered original ornamentation styles.

Academicism (1850 – ca. 1900)

A period of rapid industrial expansion took place in Germany during the latter half of the 19th century: the so-called "Gründerjahre" (founding years). This was an epoch when artistic design, particularly in the arts and crafts and in architecture, revived examples of ornaments and styles of the past. The need for decoration (which since the start of the 20th century has decreased from year to year) was acknowledged to be self-evident, but in the absence of an original style, Gothic and Baroque, and later on, Renaissance ornaments were revived. A mixture of various style periods was often deliberately made to achieve an eclectic effect. It was not until Art Nouveau appeared that a truly new style was created.

Art Nouveau (1895 – ca. 1910/1914)

At first Art Nouveau was a reaction against the mechanization and industrialization of the arts and crafts. It was thought that manual craftsmanship should offer resistance to the encroachment of technology. This counter-movement began in England, where new aesthetic principles for the arts and crafts were pursued. Art Nouveau ornamentation is based on Asiatic or folkloric plant and animal motifs predominantly found on the water surface: swans, cranes, lotus blossoms and water lilies, but also mistletoe and poppies, to mention only a few examples. Because of the influence of the Japanese woodcut on European designers, Art Nouveau ornaments may also be planar and asymmetrical.

Modernism

The decades between the First and Second World Wars were characterized by technical and rational thinking; austerity of form gained general acceptance. Yet in the so-called Art Deco movement (ca. 1920–1940), ornaments can be found which have a geometrical look and display the influences of contemporary aesthetics. In the past few years, adornment has again come into fashion in conjunction with the pop movement. Experiments are made with type, with love and peace symbols. The so-called New Orleans style of the American South also yields ornamental motifs. And once again ornament and symbol draw closer, and it is difficult to differentiate between them.

The cast ornament

Although the cast ornament is always printed, the printed ornament is not always cast. With this term we refer to adornments, embellishments, borders or any of the other names given to the cast ornament. Castings were produced in an alloy made up of lead, antimony and tin. These ornaments were sold by type foundries to printers, and even in this electronic age of photocomposition they are still available. Today, however, they are not found in compositor storage bins, but as negative stencils or as digitalized bits. If we ask what tool is used to make a cast ornament, the answer we receive is the casting instrument. But this is only one of many tools used to produce this sort of ornament. Casting serves primarily to create the die, which may be mechanically or galvanically produced. Scorper, file and burin were used well into the 19th century in making these ornaments.

It is even more interesting to learn that the basic elements of an ornament were furnished to the compositor, who then had to assemble them. The amount of talent he possessed determined the results, and quite different specimens were produced with the same elements.

Foundries supplied this kind of cast ornament in various sizes and thicknesses. It was possible in some instances to order an ornament in three or four different sizes. Today photocomposition makes possible an infinite variety of sizes.

The *vignette* (in French, "vine tendril") may consist of a representational or non-representational motif. Originally designed as book decorations and primarily used for chapter endings, the pictorial motifs were broadened to include chalices, wedding rings and other conceits which were frequently used for private invitations, announcements and on menus. The *unit figure* could be applied in the same way as a vignette, but was designed more as a repeatable figure in borders and frames. Several of these figures, such as the Aldine leaf, when repeated in a row, created a decorative border. The motif could be representational or non-representational, geometrical, interlocked or an open, continuous form.

The *row ornament*, usually a *decorative border*, was composed from a set number of single pieces. The border was first used as book decoration, above all as a chapter headpiece. It later came into general use on other printed matter.

The *cast unit* was composed of several single pieces cast into a short row ornament. It was designed for reasons of economy and was used to expedite composition for larger printing lots.

The *ornamental frame* is nothing more than a repeated border ornament. For non-geometric decor motifs a corner-piece was necessary. The *corner-piece* was supplied by type foundries along with non-geometric border ornaments. On these pieces, the decor motif was carried around the corner at a ninety-degree angle. Sometimes the compositor used a corner-piece from another motif which matched the stylistic concept.

The *fanfare* was made up of large unit figures or cast units. It served to decorate bindings or endpapers. It was also used at times on securities or stocks.

The *flourish,* an ornate rococo design which again had its origin in the Renaissance, is astonishingly suitable in combination with classical lettering, since it fits into its spirit and character. It can be found in old copperplate engravings and was rediscovered for the lithography.

The *English line,* like the flourish, developed out of copperplate engraving. One could call it the amoeba among the ornaments. This line, diminishing at both sides, may contribute a decorative element when combined with other pieces.

The integrated ornament

This ornament is not an illustration, but at most a component of an illustration. It is above all a decoration which serves a specific purpose, one that in some cases is similar to the symbol. In any case, it would be classified as belonging to the border territories we spoke of in chapter one.

The *initial* was originally a symbol. The writing masters of the Renaissance and Baroque periods understood how to entwine letter and ornamentation to such an extent that they formed an indivisible unit. In addition to this type of initial, there are of course those which employ the ornament more as a form of background decoration. Today the function of the initial is solely that of a decorative conceit.

The *fillet,* whether headpiece, tailpiece or even border, can only be called an integrated ornament if it is not an illustration, yet forms a unique part of a certain work; that is, it would not be suitable for use on another work.

The *guilloche* is the finely elaborate tracery which we find on stock certificates and bank notes, and is without doubt classifiable as an integrated ornament. It is similar to the plaited decorations we find in Dürer's work. This ornament pleases the eye with its colorfulness, achieved by the process called rainbow printing. With this printing technique, the various colors melt into each other in the manner of the rainbow. Stock certificates, securities and other legal papers are executed in this decorative style, which is usually produced by steel engraving. Similar ornamentation can be found on postage stamps, mostly on older issues.

The electronic ornament. Interactive videotex works with symbols which could be designated as pictograms. Yet these figures are not really ornaments. However, the stencil with which they are produced is called a scanning screen, and corresponds exactly to the textile screen used in silk screening. This results in strongly decorative characteristics, often so strong that they mask the symbolic content of the sign.

A completely new art has come into being with the production of electronic figures and holograms. Their curves and lines, created with a cathode ray or laser beam, are similar to those of the guilloche, but these forms signal the development of a new graphic art. The first and second German television channels (ARD and ZDF) employ figures such as these as station identifications; for commercials they are used to define the space between two TV-spots. Doubtlessly these two signals have their origin in the symbol, since they begin with a stylized eye. But most TV viewers see nothing more in them than a decoration, which together with the respective channel monogram has become an easily recognizable TV emblem.

There is not yet sufficient data on the possibilities of the hologram as a tool producing a new kind of ornamentation; at least the results so far achieved have not yet been tabulated. Yet we are sure that the hologram will go on to become a vital element in the history of the ornament in this century and beyond.

Individual ornaments

32
Non-assembled ornaments

87
Cast unit pieces assembled from
various elements

Arabesques, 16th cn.

Arabesques, 16th cn.

Vignettes in Renaissance style, ca. 1910

Row ornaments and vignettes in Renaissance style

Row ornaments with arabesque ornament, 16th cn.

Row ornaments in Renaissance style

Baroque end-piece vignettes, 17th/18th cn.

Baroque end-pieces, 17th/18th cn.

End-pieces with tendril decorations, 17th cn.

End-pieces with tendril decorations, 17th cn.

Row ornaments from the baroque period

Row ornaments from the baroque period

Baroque flourishes

Baroque flourishes

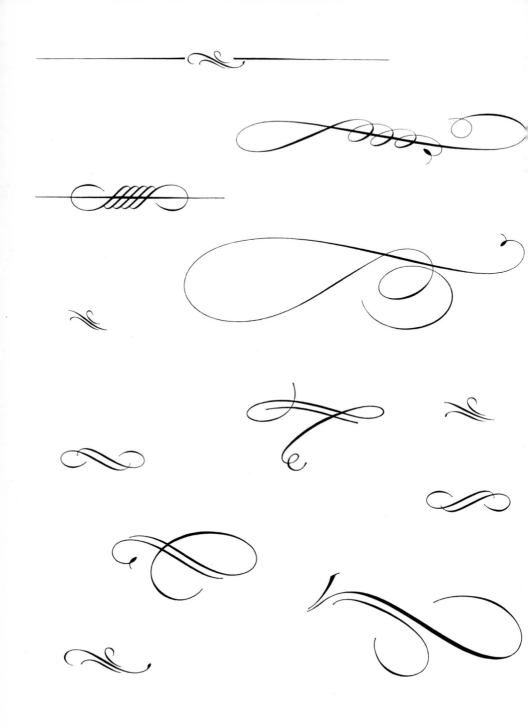

Baroque flourishes

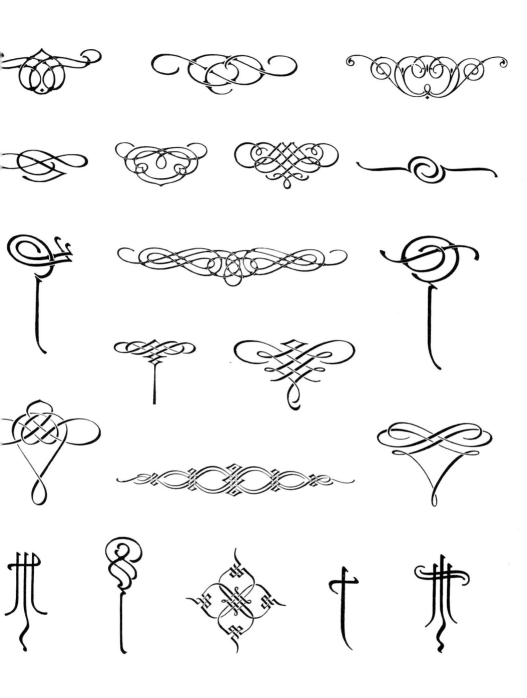

Chapter-ending pieces in Renaissance manner

47

Chapter-ending pieces in Renaissance manner

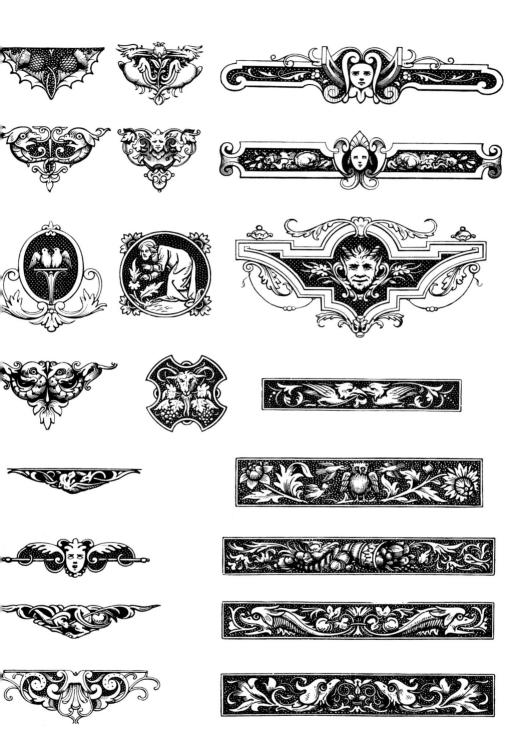

Row ornaments and end-pieces in Renaissance style, 19th cn.

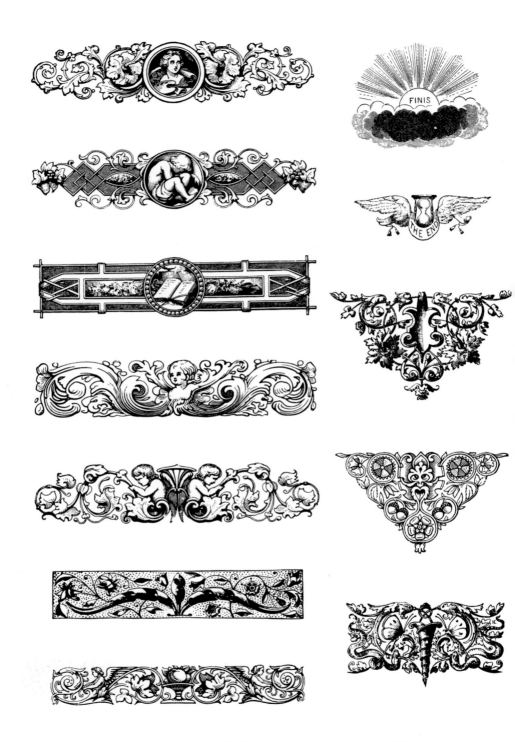

Row ornaments and end-pieces in the baroque manner, 19th cn.

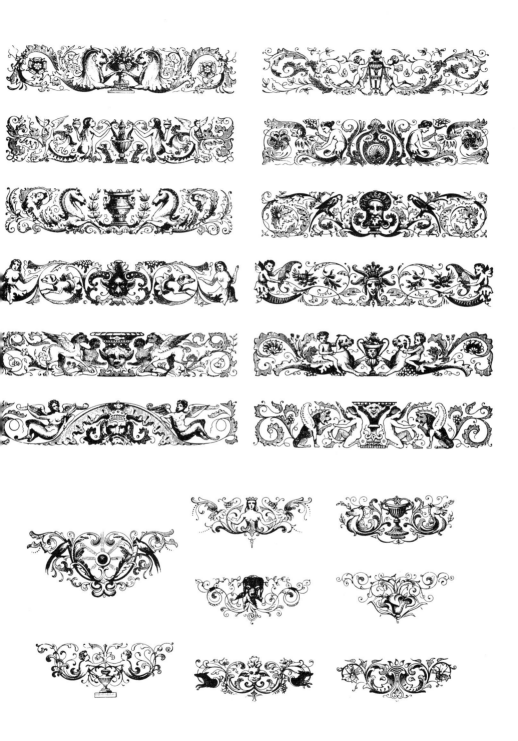

Row ornaments and end-pieces in the baroque manner, 19th cn.

Corner-pieces, end of 19th cn.

Corner-pieces, Darmstadt 1839

Vignettes, Academicism period

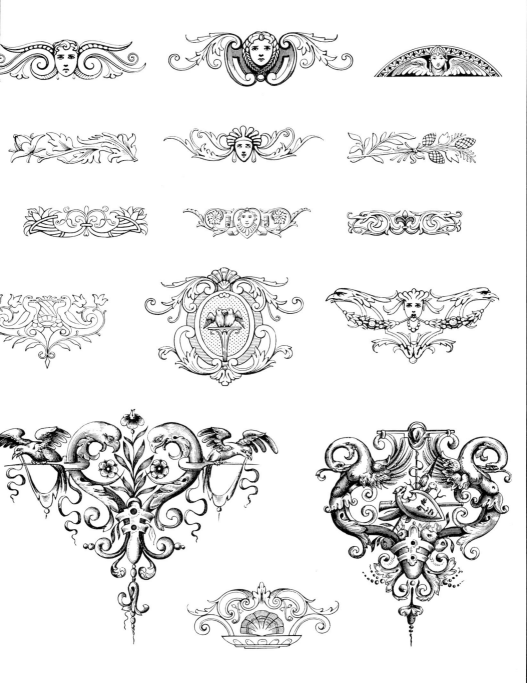

Vignettes, Academicism period

Fantasy-rosettes, Munich 1839

Edgings from the Academicism period, Berlin 1884

Edgings in Renaissance style, Berlin 1884

Row ornaments, Art Nouveau, styled on Renaissance motifs, about 1900

Row ornaments at the turn of the century

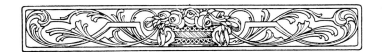

Row ornaments at the turn of the century

Vignettes for greeting cards, early 20th cn.

Chapter-ending vignettes, early 20th cn.

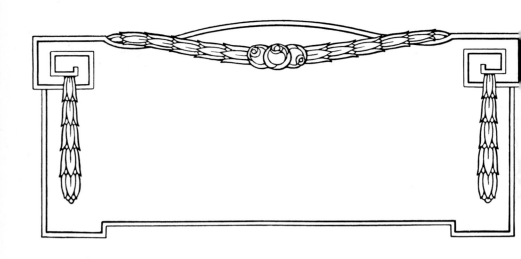

Vignettes for greeting cards, early 20th cn.

Vignettes for greeting cards, early 20th cn.

Chapter-ending vignettes, early 20th cn.

Chapter-ending vignettes, early 20th cn.

Chapter-ending vignettes, early 20th cn.

Chapter-ending vignettes from the Academicism period

Chapter-ending vignettes from the Academicism period

Vignettes, Art Nouveau. England, early 20th cn.

71

Edgings, Art Nouveau. England, early 20th cn.

Edgings, Art Nouveau. England, early 20th cn.

Edgings, Art Nouveau. England, early 20th cn.

Edgings and cartouches, Art Nouveau, early 20th cn.

Corner-pieces and edgings, Art Nouveau, early 20th cn.

Corner-pieces and edgings, Art Nouveau, early 20th cn.

Edgings and cartouches, Art Nouveau, early 20th cn.

Edgings and vignettes. Richard Grimm, about 1899

Edgings and vignettes. Richard Grimm, about 1899

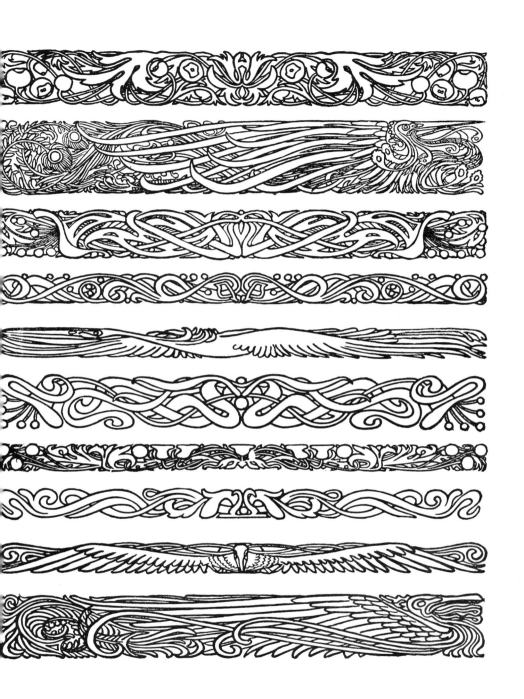

Transverse borders. Heinrich Vogeler, 1905

Vignettes. Emanuel Margold, 1910

Headpieces and end-pieces for "Die Neue Rundschau". Emil Rudolf Weiß, Berlin 1905–1907

Headpieces and end-pieces for "Die Neue Rundschau". Emil Rudolf Weiß, Berlin 1905–1907

Headpieces for "Schaffsteins Volksbücher". Emil Rudolf Weiß, Berlin, about 1905

Headpieces for "Schaffsteins Volksbücher". Emil Rudolf Weiß, Berlin, about 1905

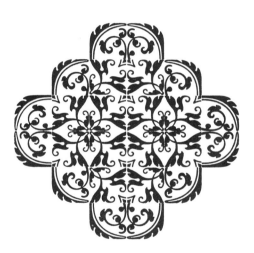

So-called Granjon arabesques, 16th cn.

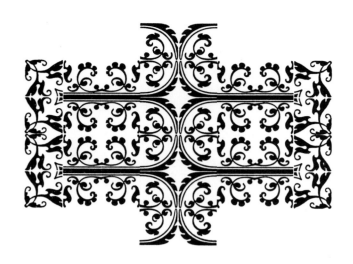

So-called Granjon arabesques, 16th cn.

Various decorative elements in rococo style. Emil Rudolf Weiß, et alii, about 1913

Typographical decorations composed from single figures. Emil Rudolf Weiß, about 1913

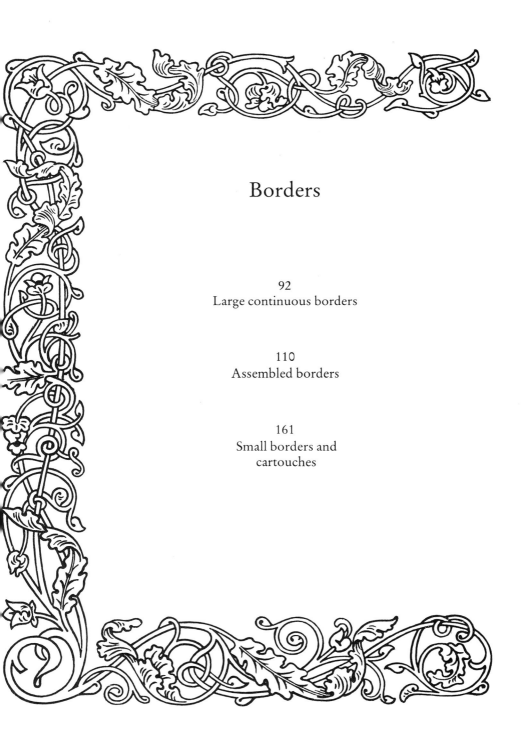

Borders

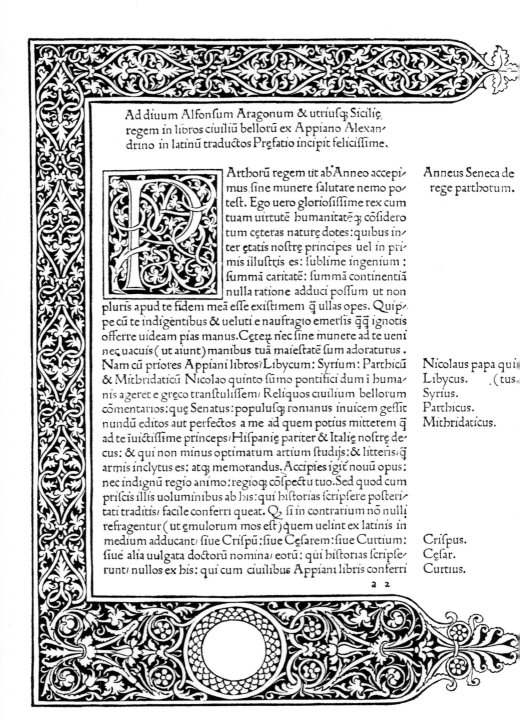

Ad diuum Alfonfum Aragonum & utriufq; Sicilie.
regem in libros ciuiliũ bellorũ ex Appiano Alexan-
drino in latinũ traductos Prefatio incipit feliciffime.

Atthorũ regem ut ab'Anneo accepi-
mus.fine munere falutare nemo po-
teft. Ego uero gloriofiffime rex cum
tuam uirtutẽ humanitatẽ๏ cõfidero
tum ceteras nature dotes:quibus inter etatis noftre principes uel in pri-
mis iilluftris es: fublime ingenium :
fummã caritatẽ: fummã continentiã
nulla ratione adduci poffum ut non
pluris apud te fidem meã effe exiftimem q̃ ullas opes. Quip-
pe cũ te indigèntibus & ueluti e nauftagio emerfis q̃q̃ ignotis
offerre uideam pias manus.Ceter๏ nec fine munere ad te ueni
nec uacuis (ut aiunt) manibus tuã maieftatẽ fum adoraturus .
Nam cũ priores Appiani libros/Libycum: Syrium: Parthicũ
& Mithridaticũ Nicolao quinto fũmo pontifici dum i huma-
nis ageret e greco tranftuliffem/ Reliquos ciuilium bellorum
cõmentarios:que Senatus:populufq๏ romanus inuicem geffit
nundũ editos aut perfectos a me ad quem potius mitterem q̃
ad te iuictiffime princeps/Hifpanie pariter & Italie noftre de-
cus: & qui non minus optimatum artium ftudijs:& litteris/q̃
armis inclytus es: atq๏ memorandus.Accipies igit̃ nouũ opus:
nec indignũ regio animo:regioq๏ cõfpectu tuo.Sed quod cum
prifcis illis uoluminibus ab his:qui hiftorias fcripfere pofteri-
tati traditis/ facile conferri queat. Q̃ fi in contrarium nõ nulli
refragentur (ut emulorum mos eft)quem uelint ex latinis in
medium adducant/ fiue Crifpũ:fiue Cefarem:fiue Curtium:
fiue alia uulgata doctorũ nomina/ eotũ: qui hiftorias fcripfe-
runt/ nullos ex his: qui cum ciuilibus Appiani libris conferri

a 2

Anneus Seneca de
rege parthotum.

Nicolaus papa qui
Libycus.   (tus.
Syrius.
Parthicus.
Mithridaticus.

Crifpus.
Cefar.
Curtius.

Title page decoration, woodcut. Erhart Ratdolt, Venice 1478

92

Prologus.

¶INCIPIT EXPOSITIO BEATI HIERONYMI
PRAESBYTERI IN PSALTERIVM. ET PRIMO
PROLOGVS EIVSDEM.

ROXIME CVM ORIGENIS
Pſalteriuʒ quod Enchiridion ille uocabat
ſtrictis & neceſſariis interpraetationibus
annotatum in cōmune legeremus: ſimul
uterqʒ depraehēdimus nonnulla eum uel
perſtrinxiſſe leuiter:uel intacta pœnitus re
liquiſſe:de quibus in alio opere latiſſime
diſputauit:quo ſcilicet non poterat rē ma
gnam breui ſermone concludere. Igitur
pro familiaritate quæ inter nos eſt:ſtudio
ſe & ſedule poſtulaſti:ut quæcūqʒ mihi di
gna memoria uidebantur ſignis quibuſ-
dam potius quá interpraetationibus ad-
notarem. Et(quod ſolent hi facere qui in
breui tabella terratum & urbium ſitus pingunt:& latiſſimas regiones in
modico ſpatio conantur oſtendere) ita in pſalterii opere latiſſimo quaſi
praeteriés aliqua perſtringerē:ut ex paucis quæ tetigiſſem intelligantur
& cætera quæ ommiſſa ſunt:quam uim habeant atqʒ rationem. Non ꝙ
putem a me poſſe dici quæ ille praeterit: ſed quo ea quæ in Thomis uel
homeliis ipſe differuit uel ego digna arbitior lectione:in hunc anguſtū
commentariolum referam. Pſalterium græcum eſt:& latine organum
dicitur:quem hebrei nablath uocant. Pſalmus dicitur:eo ꝙ a pſalte-
rio nomen accepit:uel pro ſaltandum. Quamuis Dauid omnes pſal-
mos cantaſſet:tamen omnes pſalmi in perſona chriſti pertinent:& qui
praetitulati eſſe non uidentur:apud hebreos pro uno pſalmo habentur.
Nam per titulum intelligitur uniuſcuiuſqʒ pſalmi intellectus. Quid eſt
titulus niſi clauis?(Vt ita dixerim) in domo nō igreditur niſi per clauim
ita & uniuſcuiuſqʒ pſalmi intellectus per clauem:hoc eſt per titulum in
telligitur:in cuius perſona cantatur:aut in perſona chriſti:aut in perſona
eccleſiæ:aut in perſona prophetæ.

aA A z

Border edging, metal engraving. Giovanni and Gregorio da Gregoriis, Venice 1498

Specimen with border. Conrad Fyner, Urach 1481

Terentius cum
quinq3 cómen-
tis: vz Dona-
ti: Guido-
nis: Cal-
phur.
Ascensu ꝫ Seruii.

⸿ Cum gratia: vt pa-
tet in suis priuilegijs.

Title page ornamentation and border. L. Soardi, Venice 1499

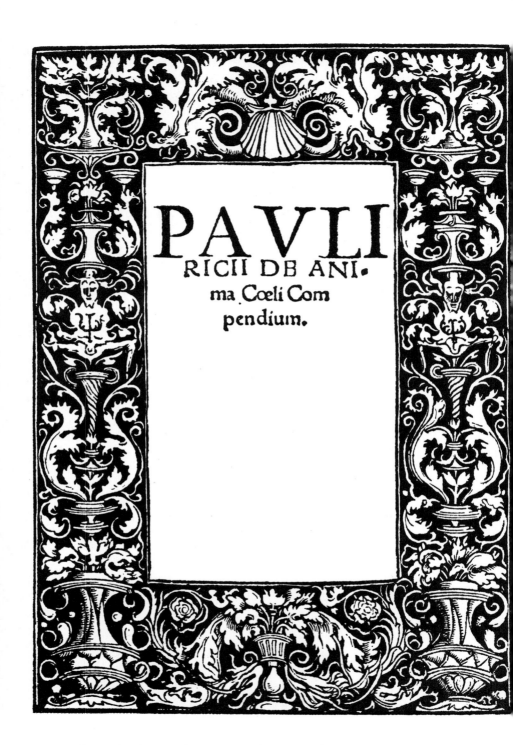

PAVLI
RICII DB ANI.
ma Coeli Com
pendium.

Title page border, woodcut. Sigismund Grimm and Max Wirsung, Augsburg 1519

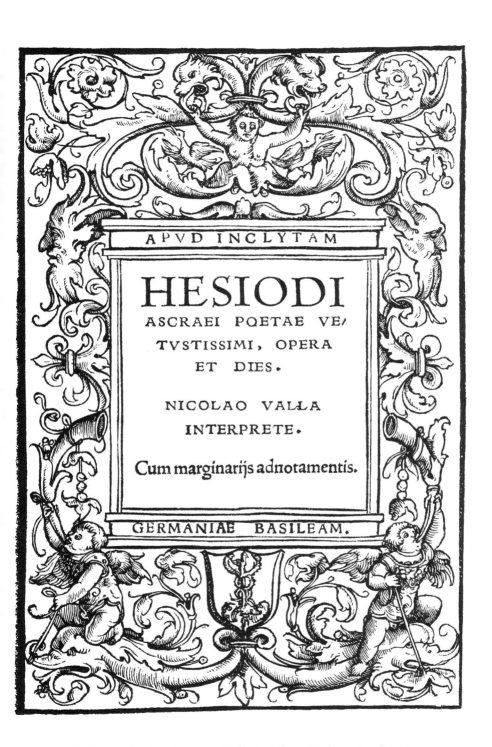

APVD INCLYTAM

HESIODI
ASCRAEI POETAE VE/
TVSTISSIMI, OPERA
ET DIES.

NICOLAO VALLA
INTERPRETE.

Cum marginarijs adnotamentis.

GERMANIAE BASILEAM.

Title page border after Hans Holbein. Johann Frobens, Basel 1518

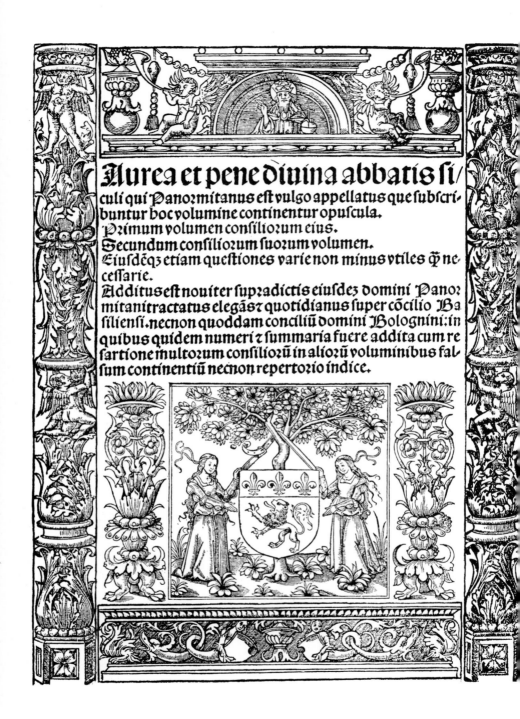

French book make-up, specimen, 16th cn.

Title page border. Daniel Hopfer, early 16th cn.

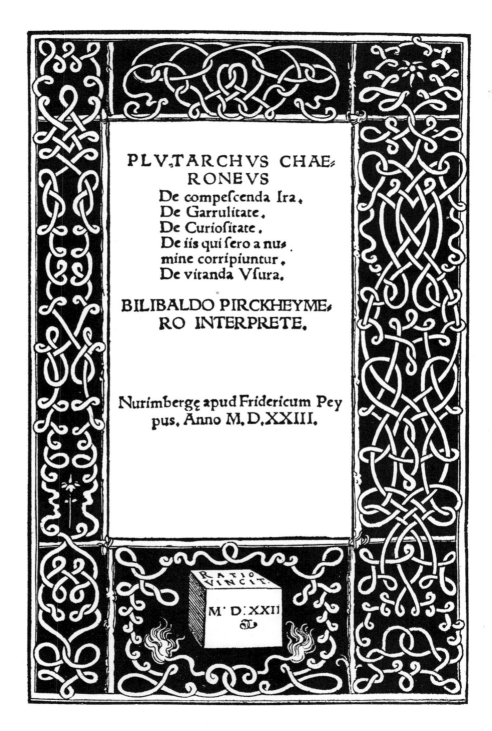

Title page border, woodcut by Albrecht Dürer. Friedrich Peypus, 1523

Title page border specimen, printing catalogue, Vincent Figgins, London 1815

Border edging in Renaissance style, Berlin 1884

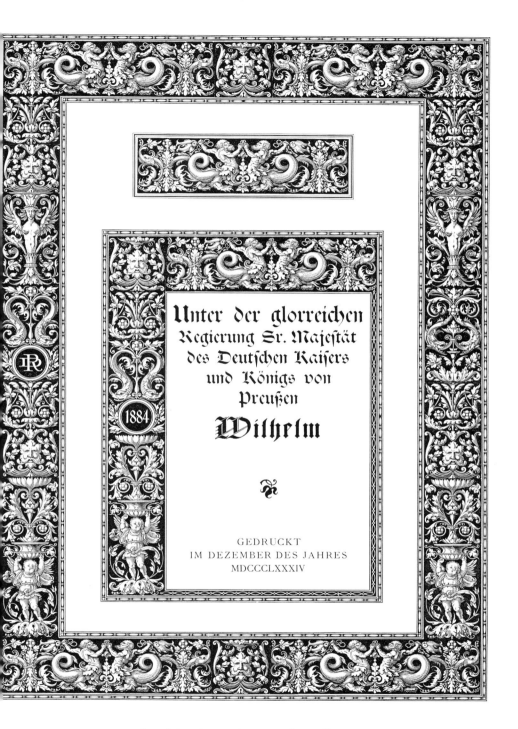

Unter der glorreichen
Regierung Sr. Majestät
des Deutschen Kaisers
und Königs von
Preußen

Wilhelm

GEDRUCKT
IM DEZEMBER DES JAHRES
MDCCCLXXXIV

Border edgings in Renaissance style, Berlin 1884

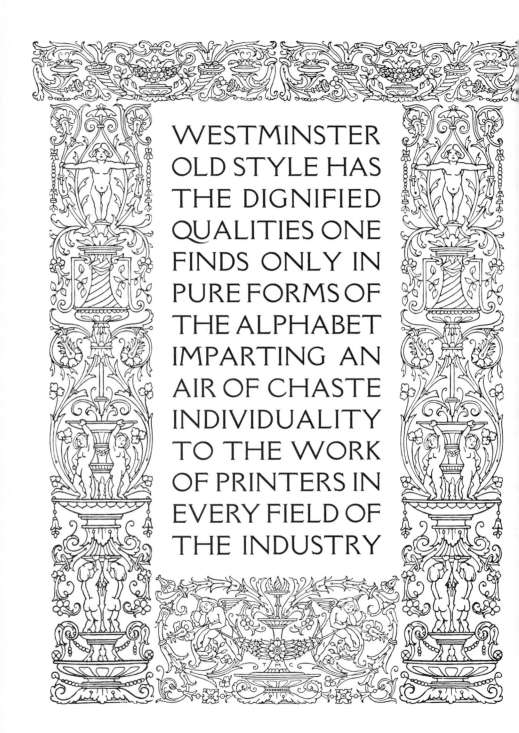

WESTMINSTER
OLD STYLE HAS
THE DIGNIFIED
QUALITIES ONE
FINDS ONLY IN
PURE FORMS OF
THE ALPHABET
IMPARTING AN
AIR OF CHASTE
INDIVIDUALITY
TO THE WORK
OF PRINTERS IN
EVERY FIELD OF
THE INDUSTRY

Border in the so-called Westminster style

Title page border. Albert Knab, 1903

Title page border. Paul Bürck, 1900

Title page border. Carl Weidemeyer, 1909

Border in Art Nouveau style, early 20th cn.

Border, plaited and woven, 19th cn.

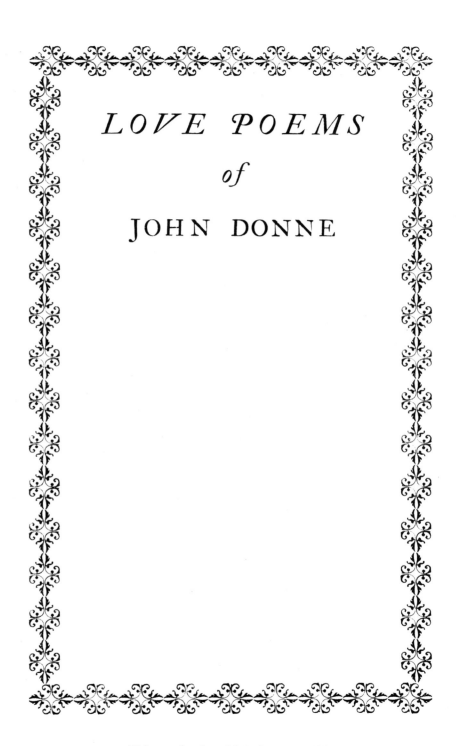

LOVE POEMS

of

JOHN DONNE

Title page border with arabesques, 1639

Christliche Leich-predig/

Von deme / wem

wir beydes leben vnd
sterben sollen.

Gehalten Sontags den 23. Apr. An. 1654.
in der Pfarkirchen des Münsters
zu Basel/

Bey Christlicher vnd ansehnlicher
bestattung / des Ehrenvesten-vnd
Vorgeachten Herren

Johann Jacob Genathen/
Burgers - vnd Buchtruckers daselb-
sten.

Vnd auff begeren in Truck verfertiget/
Von
M. Samuele Grynæo, Pfarrer
zu St. Leonhard.

Getruckt zu Basel/
Bey Johann Jacob Genath/
Sel. Erben.

Title page border with arabesques, Basel 1654

111

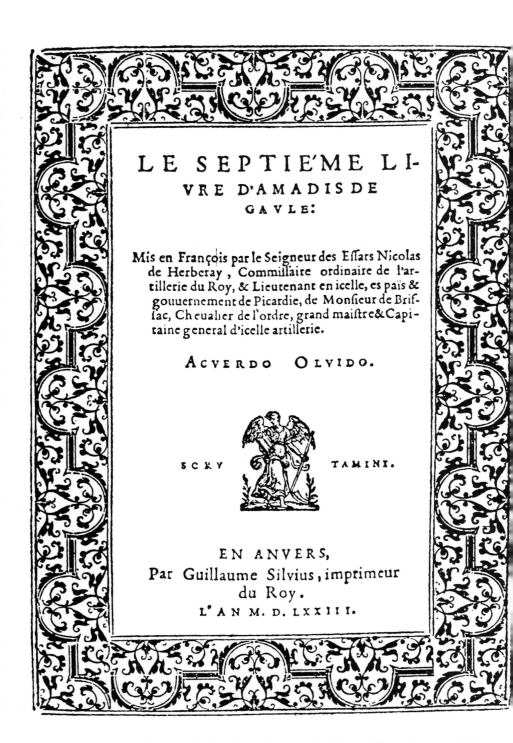

LE SEPTIE'ME LI-
VRE D'AMADIS DE
GAVLE:

Mis en François par le Seigneur des Essars Nicolas
de Herberay , Commissaire ordinaire de l'artillerie du Roy, & Lieutenant en icelle, es païs &
gouuernement de Picardie, de Monsieur de Bris-
sac, Cheualier de l'ordre, grand maistre & Capi-
taine general d'icelle artillerie.

ACVERDO   OLVIDO.

SCKV   TAMINI.

EN ANVERS,
Par Guillaume Silvius, imprimeur
du Roy.
L'AN M. D. LXXIII.

Cast title page border with Granjon arabesques. Guillaume Silvius, Antwerp 1573

Title page border with arabesques, 16th cn.

Title page border with Granjon arabesques, 16th cn.

Title page border with arabesques

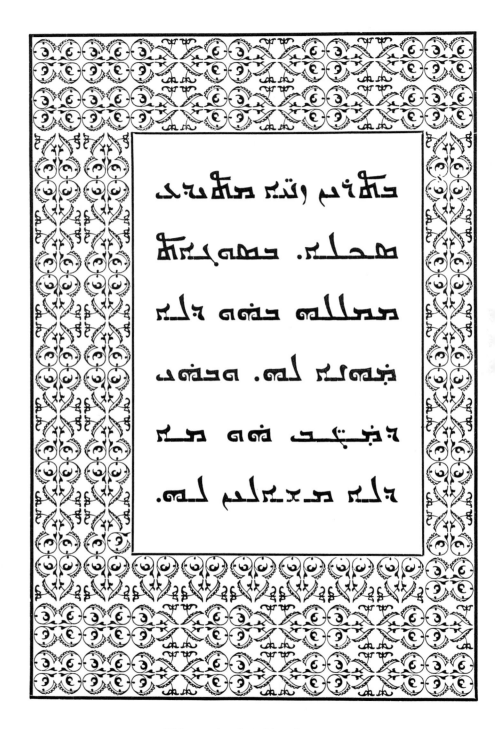

ܟܬܒܐ ܕܬܪܝܢ ܕܡܠܟܐ ܕܚܝܐ
ܠܡܘܫܐ ܫܒܝܩܝܢ ܘܓܪܡܐ
ܕܐܚܝܕ ܒܗܘܢ ܠܡܠܟܐ
ܒܓܘ ܠܗ ܘܥܒܕܘ ܬܪܝܢ
ܪܐܗ ܗܘ ܚܙܝܒ̈ܐ ܗܘ
ܠܗ ܘܪܚܝܠ ܡܠܝܟܐ ܠܗ.

Title page border with arabesques

116

Title page border with arabesques

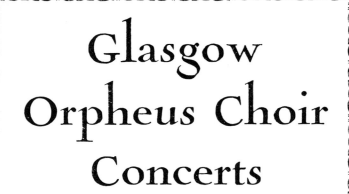

Glasgow
Orpheus Choir
Concerts
1923

Conductor

HUGH S. ROBERTON

ST. ANDREW'S HALL

Title page border with arabesques

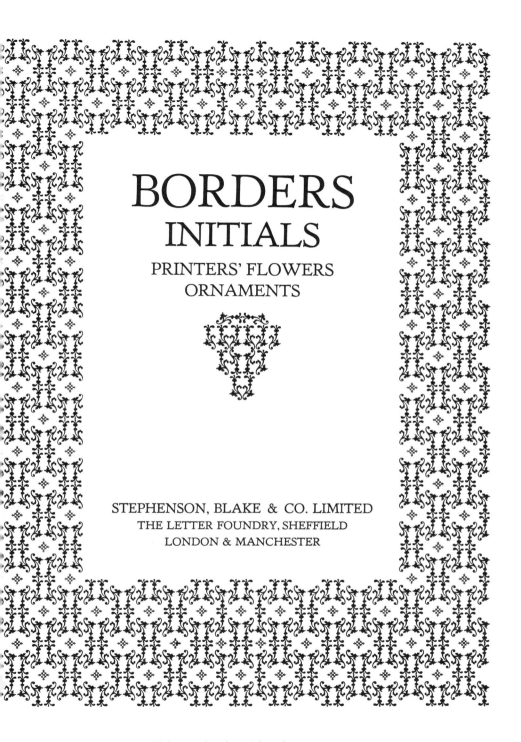

BORDERS
INITIALS
PRINTERS' FLOWERS
ORNAMENTS

STEPHENSON, BLAKE & CO. LIMITED
THE LETTER FOUNDRY, SHEFFIELD
LONDON & MANCHESTER

Title page border with arabesques

119

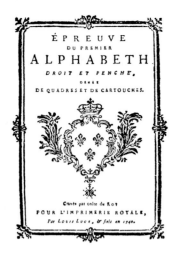

Title page borders. Pierre-Simon Fournier the younger and others, 1742

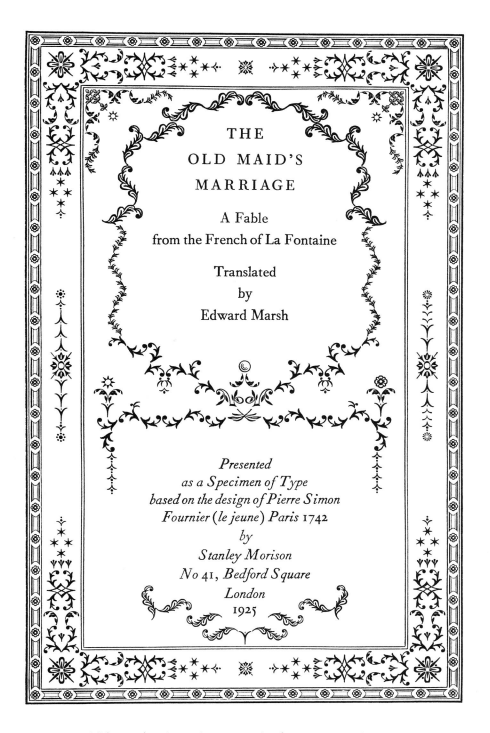

THE
OLD MAID'S
MARRIAGE

A Fable
from the French of La Fontaine

Translated
by
Edward Marsh

*Presented
as a Specimen of Type
based on the design of Pierre Simon
Fournier (le jeune) Paris 1742
by
Stanley Morison
No 41, Bedford Square
London
1925*

Title page by Pierre-Simon Fournier the younger, Paris 1742

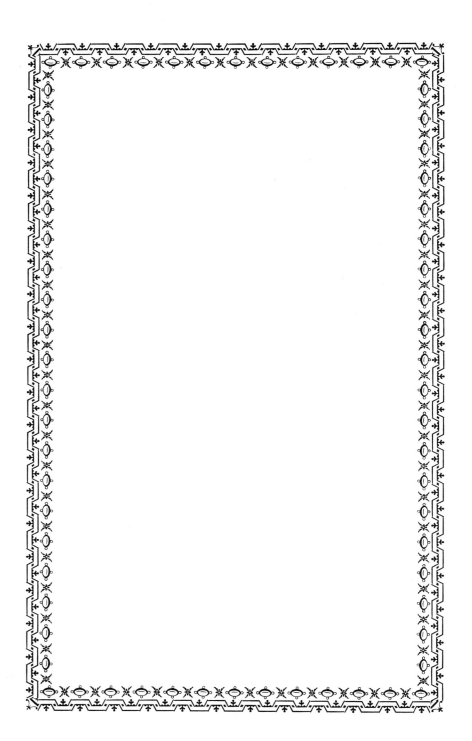

Border with rosettes. Holland, 1748

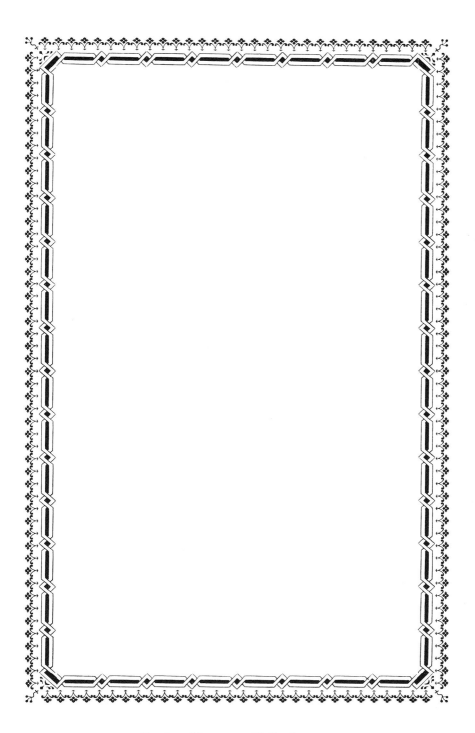

Border with rosettes. Holland, 1748

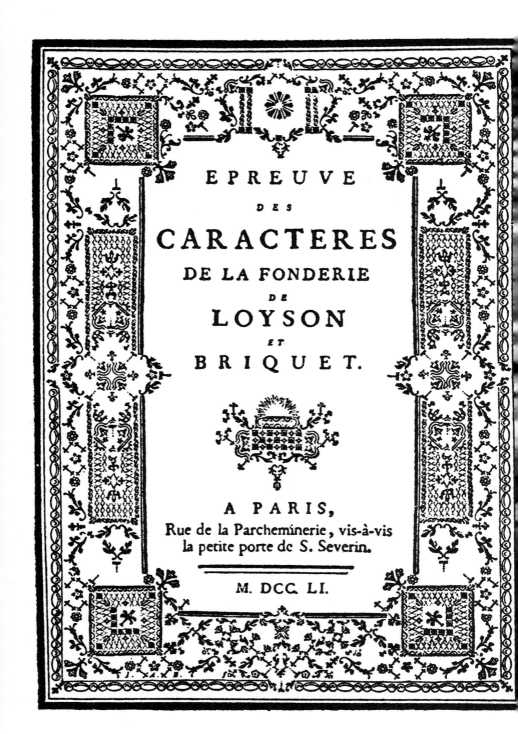

Title page from Loyson et Briquet, Paris 1751

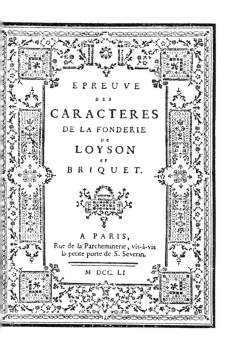

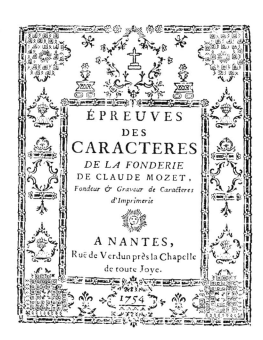

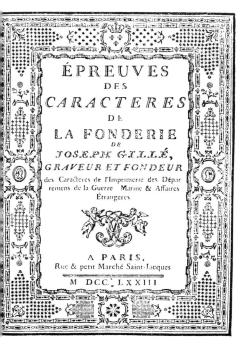

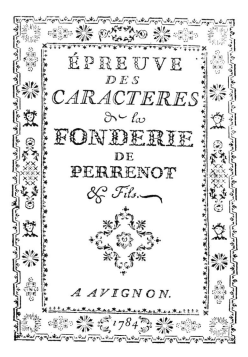

Various title pages, France, 1751–1784

Cette Fonderie de Caractéres s'aug=
mentera de tems en tems de toute forte
des beaux & nouveaux Caractéres, &
nous nous efforcerons de la mettre au
plus-haut degré de Perfection; nous n'y
épargnerons ni fraix ni peine, pour
faire paroître LE TRES-NOBLE ART DE
L'IMPRIMERIE *dans fon plus - grand*
Eclat , & pour mettre NÔTRE VILLE,
comme L'UNIQUE MERE DE CET ART,
dans fon premier Luftre.

Si quelques Savans aù Profeffeurs
auront envie de faire fondre DES CA-
RACTERES DES LANGUES ORIENTALES
pour l'Impreffion des Ouvrages, nous
fommes pièts à leur ordre de les apièter
le plus-correctement , qu'on les puiffe
foûhaiter.

Outre l'Augmentation , qu'on voit
depuis l'année 1748 jufques aujourdhui
dans cette Epreuve , nous avons encore
en=

Specimen sheet with border, 1757

Amsterdam den   17

Insonders Hochgeehrter Herr!

Dieses dienet zum beliebigen
Aviso, daß wir an dero geehrtesten
adresse dato abgesandt haben, die
nachfolgenden Bücher mit

Wir bitten hiemit, nach Statt
geben glücklicher Zukunft und Emp=
fang, dieselbigen weiter an Herren

zu befördern, die Unkosten auff
denen Büchern nach zu nehmen,
und uns von den erfolgten Transito
Bericht zu geben; und verharren
nach erlaßung in die Allerhöch=
sten obhuth

Specimen sheet with border, 1768

EULOGY
OF PIERRE SIMON
FOURNIER LE JEUNE

·❮❮━━━◈━━━❯·

Pierre Simon Fournier, engraver and type-
cutter, was born in Paris on 16th September,
1712, of parents whose probity amply made up
for a lack of property which fortune had refused
to them.

His father, Jean-Claude Fournier, learnt foundry work in Paris from Mr. Cott[1], whom he left
at an early age to go to La Flèche and then re-
turned to Paris; in 1698 he entered with the widow
of Guillaume Le Bé, third of a memorable name
in typography. This lady had remained a widow
with four daughters, whose support Fournier
soon became and whose house he conducted for
more than thirty years with a very uncommon
disinterestedness and zeal. He finally married one
of his compatriots, by whom he had three daughters, who are as many models of virtue, and who
are the principal consolation of this respected
mother; he also had six sons by her, of whom
three died at an early age. Fournier's eldest son

---

[1] The son of this Mr. Cott had commenced a great
work on his art, of which only a few sheets were printed.

Foreword, eulogy of Pierre-Simon Fournier the younger, 1770

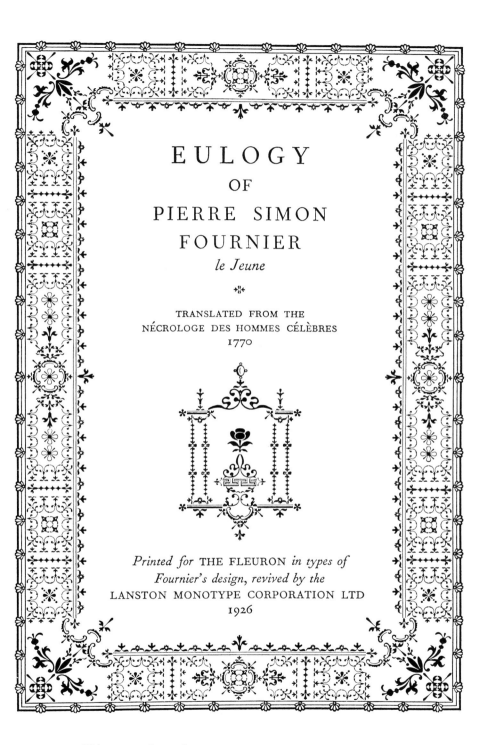

EULOGY

OF

PIERRE SIMON FOURNIER

le Jeune

❖

TRANSLATED FROM THE
NÉCROLOGE DES HOMMES CÉLÈBRES
1770

Printed for THE FLEURON *in types of
Fournier's design, revived by the*
LANSTON MONOTYPE CORPORATION LTD
1926

Title page, eulogy of Pierre-Simon Fournier the younger, 1770

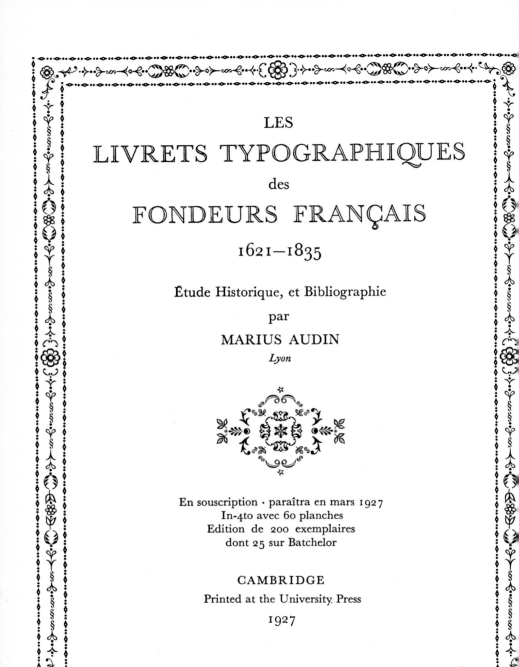

LES
LIVRETS TYPOGRAPHIQUES
des
FONDEURS FRANÇAIS
1621—1835

Étude Historique, et Bibliographie

par

MARIUS AUDIN

Lyon

En souscription · paraîtra en mars 1927
In-4to avec 60 planches
Edition de 200 exemplaires
dont 25 sur Batchelor

CAMBRIDGE
Printed at the University Press

1927

Title page border in rococo style, France, 18th cn.

Title page border in rococo style, France, 18th cn.

Non dubito fore plerosque, Attice, qui hoc genus fcripturae leve et non fatis dignum fummorum virorum perfonis judicent, cum relatum legent, quis muficam docuerit Epaminondam, aut in ejus virtutibus commemorari faltaffe eum commode, fcienterque tibiis cantaffe. BCDFGHIJ KLMOPQRSTUV WXYZ 1234567890

Title page border, Holland, 1772

Text Oud Geſchreeven.

(decorative alphabet specimen)

Auguſtijn Oud Geſchreeven.

(calligraphic French text specimen)

Henry par la Grace de Dieu/ Roy
de France et de Pologne/ Comte de Pro=
vence/ Forcalquier/ et Terres adiacentes/
au Seneſchal de Provence/ ou ſon Lieute=
nant au ſiege de Marſeille/ ſalut. Nr cher
et bien aimé Honoré Ramban d/ habitant de la=
dite Ville/ nous a fait dire et remonſtrer/ que
des long tems Jlſ eſt exercé à enſeigner les
premieres Lettres. En quoy Jl a reu=
du tel ſoin et Diligence/ quil en eſt demeuré
en extreme contentement à tous ceux à qui il
les a appriſe: ayant pour la commodité d'un
chacun qui vou dra apprendre de Lui/ et pour
la ſienne auſſi/ compoſé un Alphabet
de quelques characteres/ qui pourront ſervir
gran dement à ſoulager les Perſonnes/ meſ=
mes les petyts Enfants.

(decorative alphabet specimen)

Dit laatſte Geſchreeven Schrift is geſneden voor den vermaarden Boekdruk-
ker Chriſtoffel Plantyn te Antwerpen, door Ameet Tavernier, Letterſnyder.

Specimen sheet with border, Christoffel Plantyn, Antwerp 1768

133

Title page of a specimen catalogue. Wilhelm Haas, Basel 1772

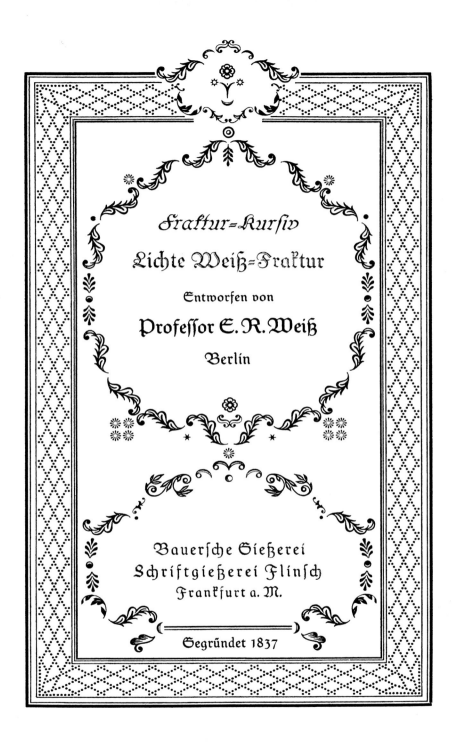

Specimen sheet in rococo style. Emil Rudolf Weiß, about 1910

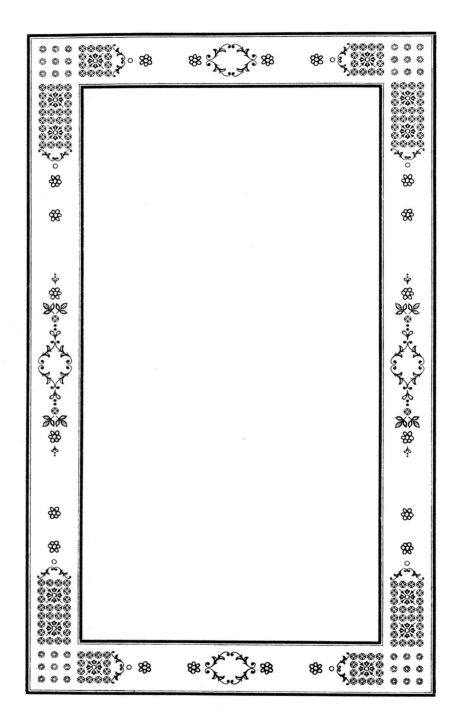

Specimen sheet in rococo style. Emil Rudolf Weiß, Berlin 1913

GOETHE

Clavigo

Illustriert von

G. von Seckendorff

Erster Druck

der

Marées-Gesellschaft

1918

Specimen sheet in rococo style. Emil Rudolf Weiß, 1918

Specimen sheet in rococo style. Emil Rudolf Weiß, 1912

Title page border in rococo style, early 20th cn.

Border in temple form. Academicism, Munich 1839

Border in temple form. Academicism, Munich 1839

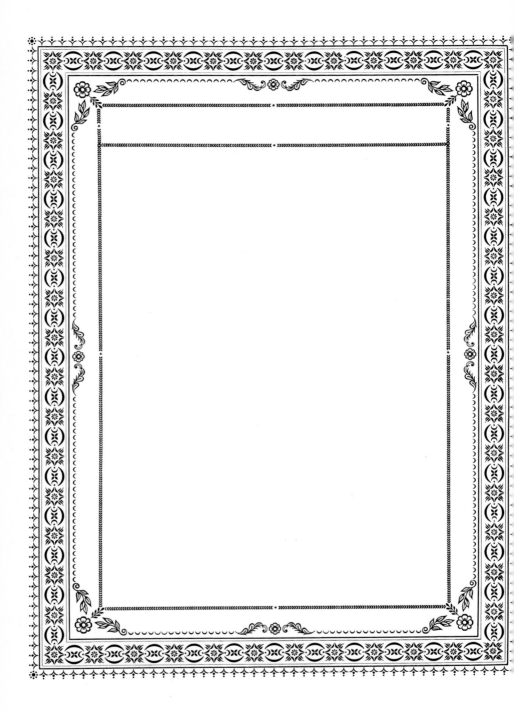

Title page border in rococo style, early 20th cn.

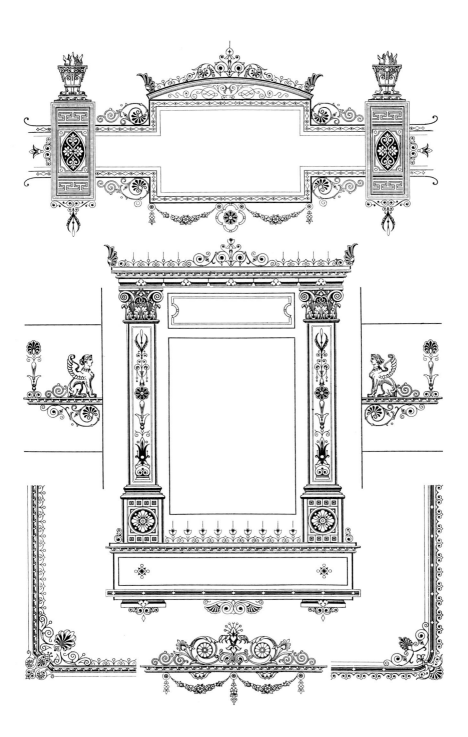

Academicistic borders. J. G. Schelter & Giesecke, about 1900

Border. Peter Behrens, 1908

Border and row ornaments. Peter Behrens, 1908

KUNST-RÄUME
HEINZ SONDE
MAGDEBURG

Mitte Januar des nächſten Jahres eröffnen wir eine Sonderausſtellung von neueren Radierungen deutſcher Künſtler. Den Vordergrund bilden die großen Folgen von radierten Blättern Max Klingers: Paraphraſe über den Verluſt eines Handſchuhs, Vom Tode I und vom Tode II, Rettung Ovidiſcher Opfer, ſodann noch etwa zwanzig kleine Einzelblätter des Meiſters. Inhaltlich ſchließen ſich an Alois Kolb und Otto Greiner mit reichhaltigen größeren Sammlungen zum Teil faſt unbekannter Drucke.

Border and row ornaments. Peter Behrens, 1908

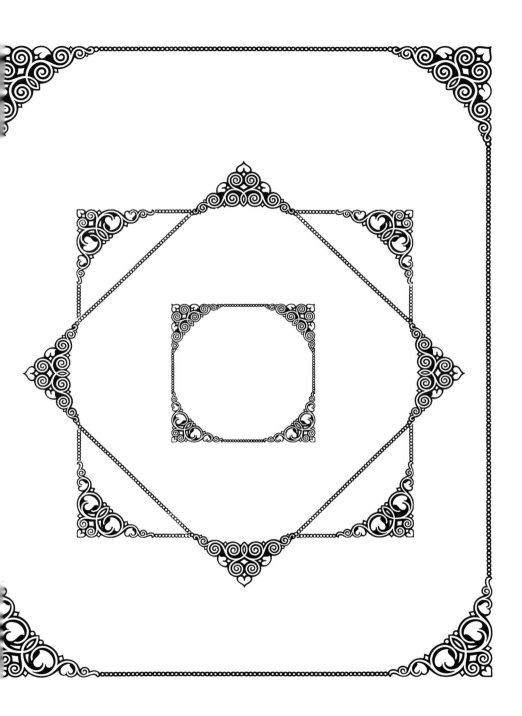

Borders and decorative corner-pieces. Friedrich Wilhelm Kleukens, about 1910

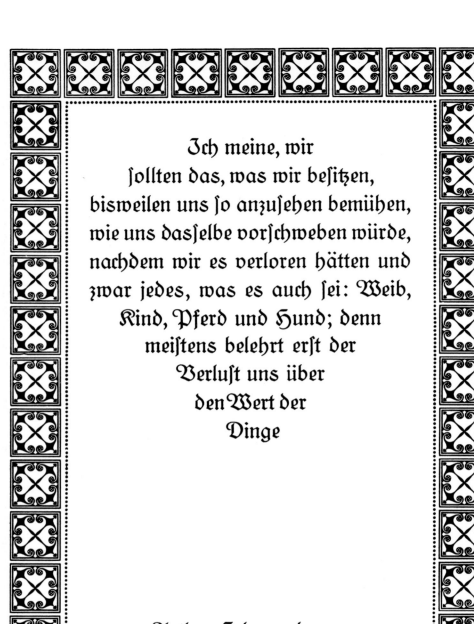

Ich meine, wir
sollten das, was wir besitzen,
bisweilen uns so anzusehen bemühen,
wie uns dasselbe vorschweben würde,
nachdem wir es verloren hätten und
zwar jedes, was es auch sei: Weib,
Kind, Pferd und Hund; denn
meistens belehrt erst der
Verlust uns über
den Wert der
Dinge

Arthur Schopenhauer

Title page border. Friedrich Wilhelm Kleukens, 1913

SCHRIFTGIESSEREI
D·STEMPEL
AG·FRANKFURT AM MAIN·SÜD

Unter Mitarbeit der bedeutendsten graph. Künstler
haben wir eine reiche Auswahl von Neuheiten für
Reklame und Akzidenz in Schriften und Schmuck
geschaffen. Interessenten stehen wir jederzeit mit
Proben unserer Erzeugnisse zur Verfügung. Wir
fabrizieren in eigener, der Neuzeit entsprechend ein-
gerichteter Messinglinienfabrik Messingmaterial jeder
Art für alle Buchdruckzwecke und legen besonderes
Gewicht auf erstkl. Rohmaterial. Unsere Galvanopl.
Anstalt liefert druckfertige Galvanos in Kupfer- oder
Nickelstahlniederschlag. * Höchste Auszeichnungen

Title page of type foundry catalogue of D. Stempel, Frankfurt 1913

Border in rococo style of the Monotype Corp., London 1926

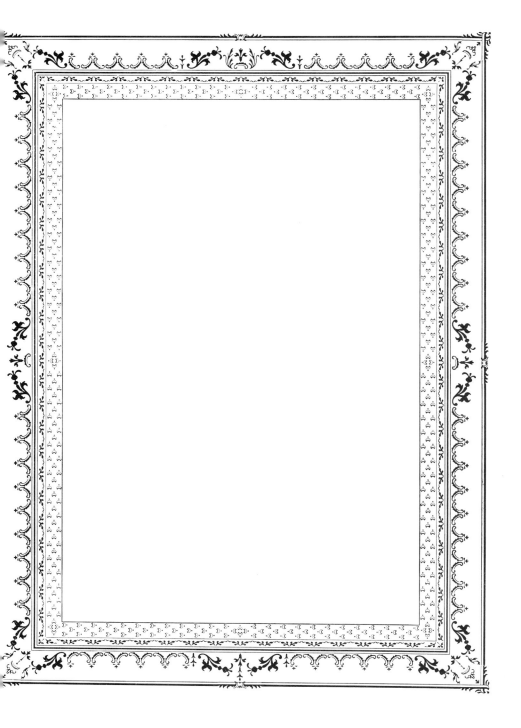

Border in rococo style of the Monotype Corp., London 1926

Border in rococo style of the Monotype Corp., London 1926

152

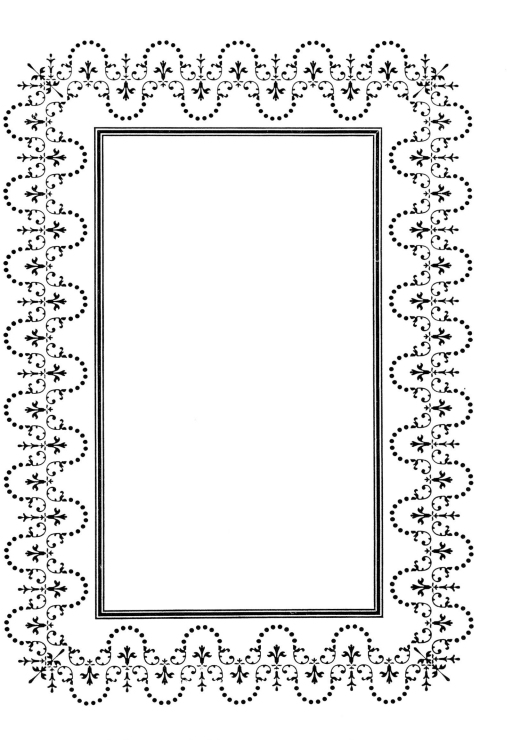

Border in rococo style of the Monotype Corp., London 1926

Border in rococo style of the Monotype Corp., London 1926

Border in rococo style of the Monotype Corp., London 1926

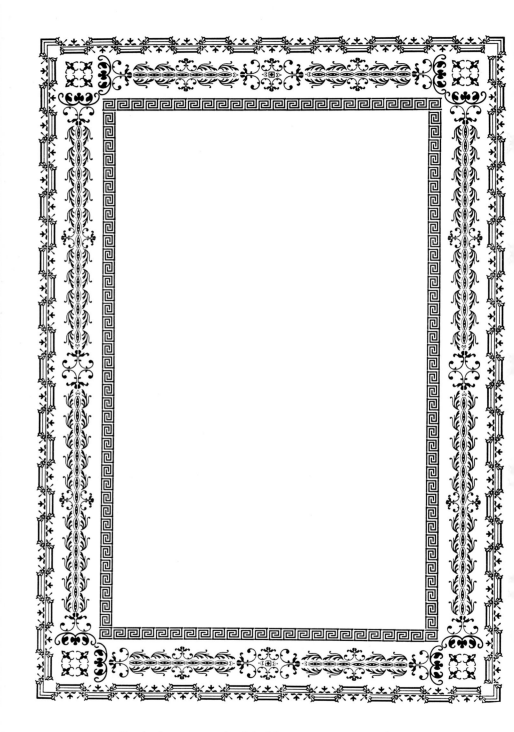

Border in rococo style of the Monotype Corp., London 1926

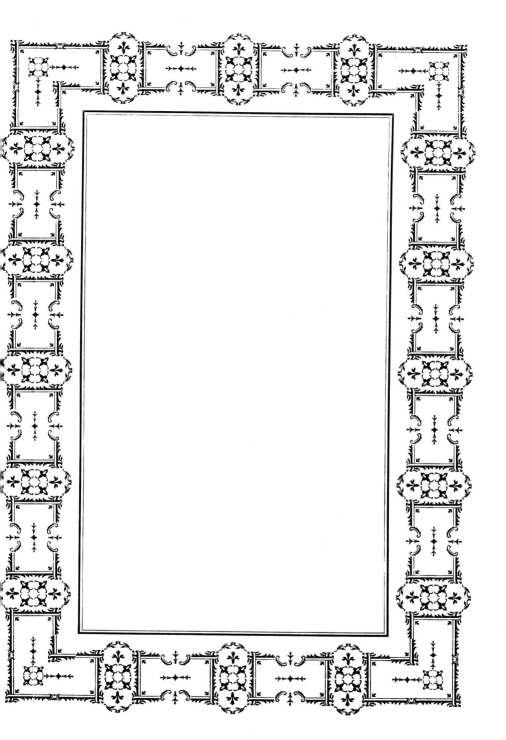

Border in rococo style of the Monotype Corp., London 1926

Border of the Monotype Corp., London 1926

Border of the Monotype Corp., London 1926

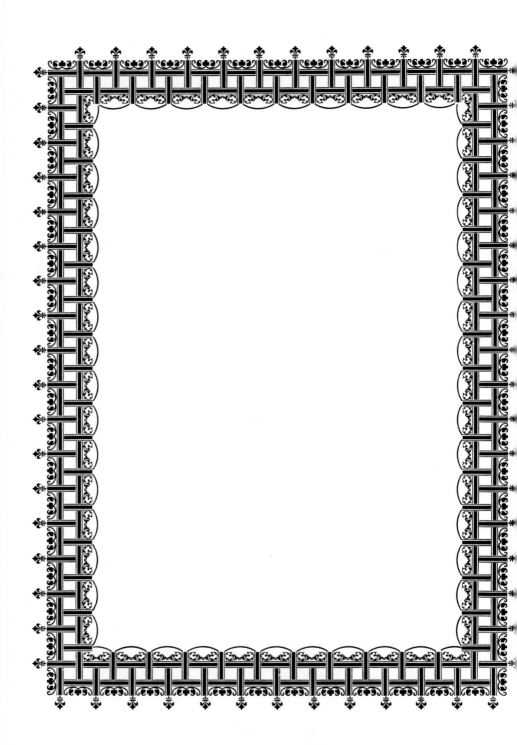

Border of the Monotype-Corp., London 1926

EX-LIBRIS

ODYSSEUM

∴

F.Q.W.

CIREDERF
DRAW

QUIXOTE'S
LODGE
HIS BOOK

EX-
LIBRIS

DODY
DAVI-
DOFF

THIS BOOK
IS FROM
THE
TURQUOISE
BED-ROOM
OF
DRAFTY
CASTLE

Borders in rococo style of the Monotype Corp.

Cartouches. Academicism, about 1870

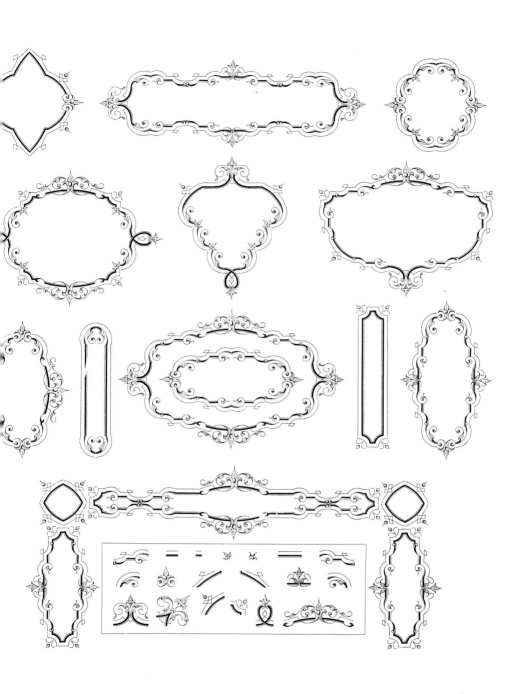

Cartouches. Academicism, about 1870

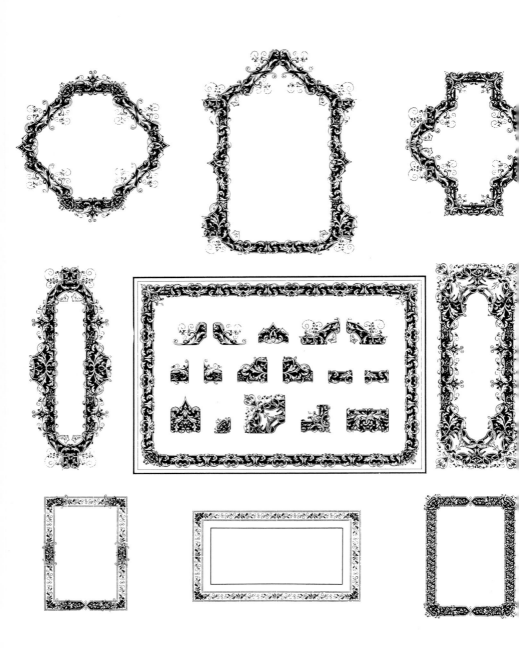

Borders and cartouches from various stylistic elements, 19th cn.

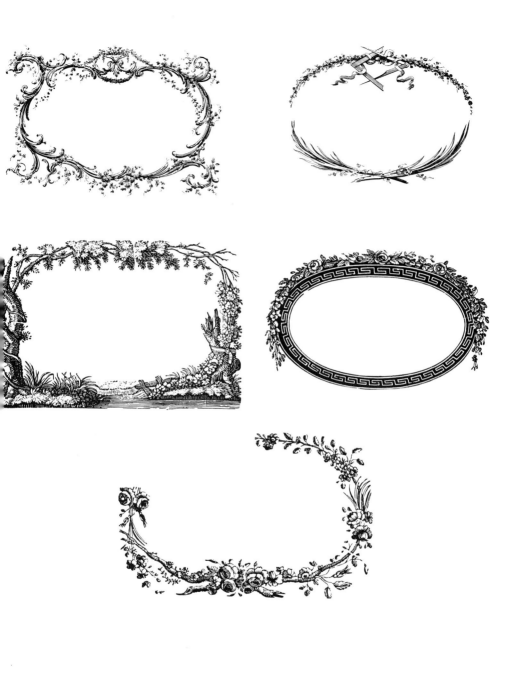

Borders and cartouches from various stylistic elements, 19th cn.

Borders and cartouches from various stylistic elements, 19th cn.

Borders and cartouches from various stylistic elements, 19th cn.

Borders and cartouches from various stylistic elements, 19th cn.

Borders and cartouches from various stylistic elements, 19th cn.

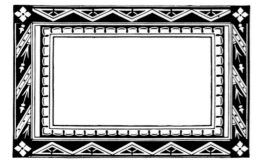 

Borders and cartouches from various stylistic elements, 19th cn.

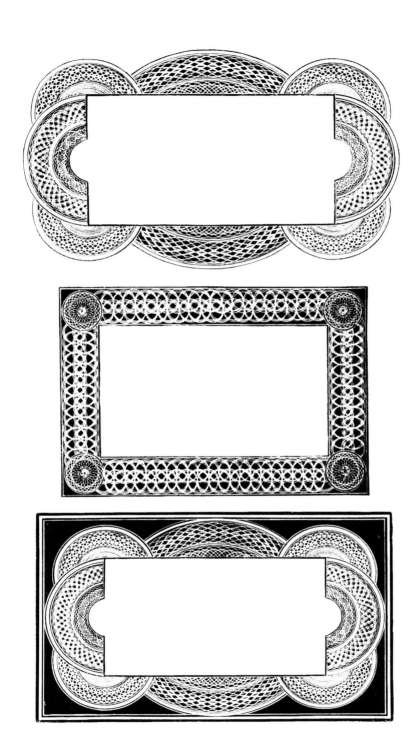

Guilloched cartouches, 19th cn.

Cartouches in the Renaissance style with scallop- and scrollwork. Berlin 1884

Cartouches in the Renaissance style with scallop- and scrollwork. Berlin 1884

Headpieces for "Die Neue Rundschau". Emil Rudolf Weiß, Berlin 1905–1907

Cartouches. Paul Bürck and others, 1899–1903

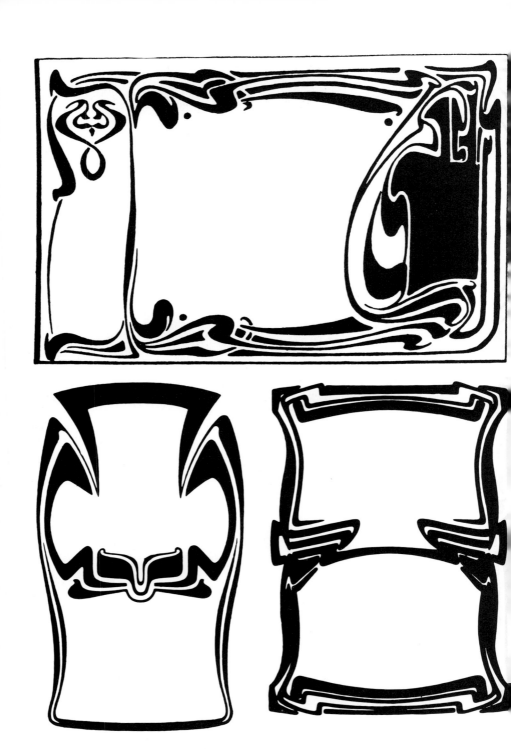

Cartouches. Henry van de Velde, about 1899 and 1897

Cartouches, from l. to r.: anon., 1905; Y. Storck, 1903; O. Eckmann, 1900; J. V. Cissarz, 1900

P. Behrens, 1901; O. Eckmann, ca. 1900; anon., ca. 1900; P. Behrens, 1900

Row and border pieces

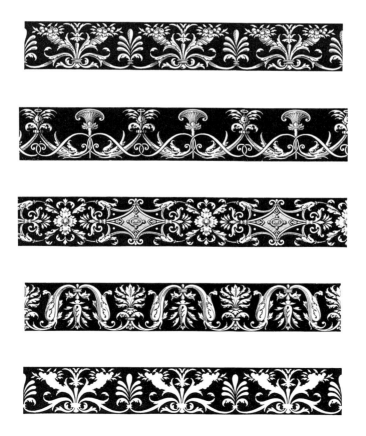

Vil dünt jnn dorßeyt ßye beßarren,
Vnd zießen vast eyn schweren karrßen,
Dort würt der recßt wag naßer faren

võ dẽ weg der sellikeit
Gott laßt eyn narren nit verston
Syn wunder / die er hat getßon
Vnd tåglicß důt / dar vmß verdyrßt
Gar mancßer narr / der zittlicß styrßt

Illustration for Sebastian Brant's "Ship of Fools", Albrecht Dürer, Basel 1494

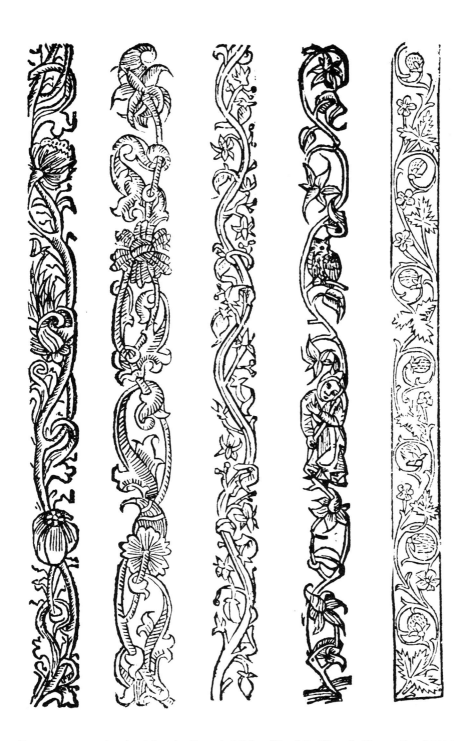

Row ornamentation for Sebastian Brant's "Ship of Fools", Albrecht Dürer, Basel 1494

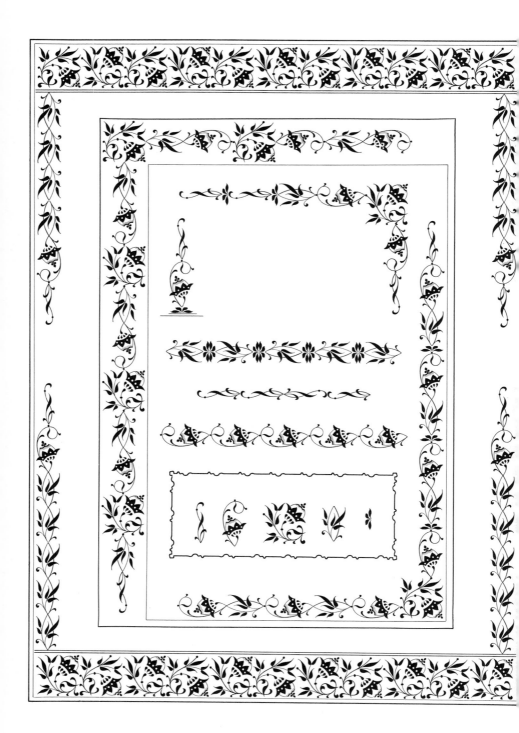

Row ornaments with arabesque motifs in 16th cn. style

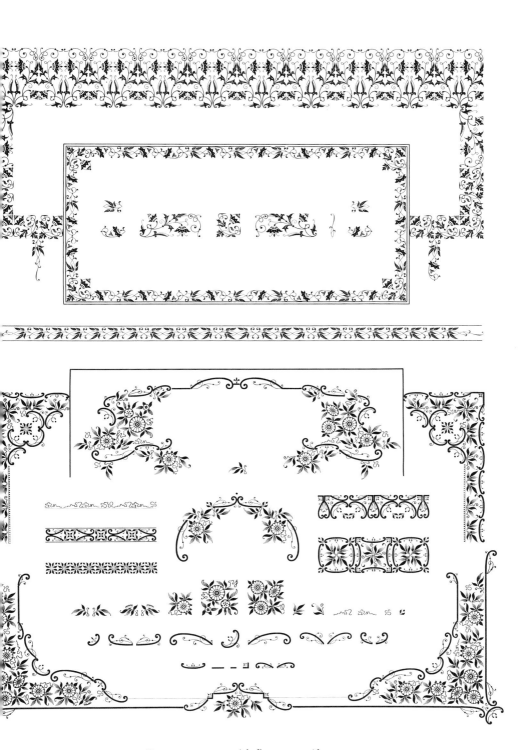

Row ornaments with flower motifs

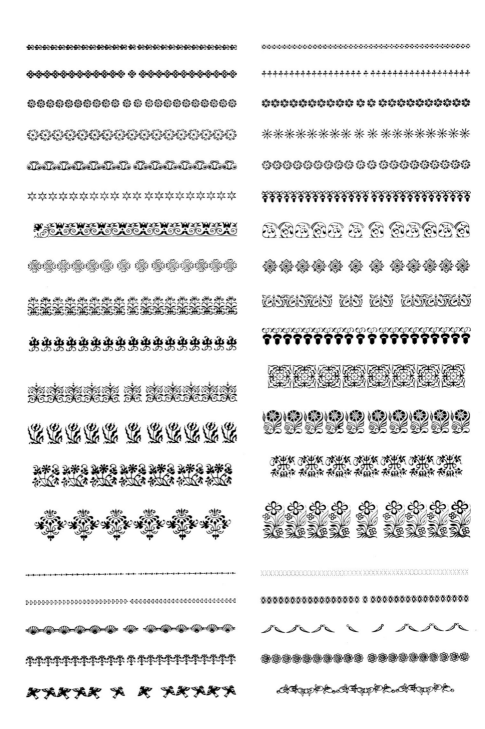

Row ornaments in rococo style, 18th cn.

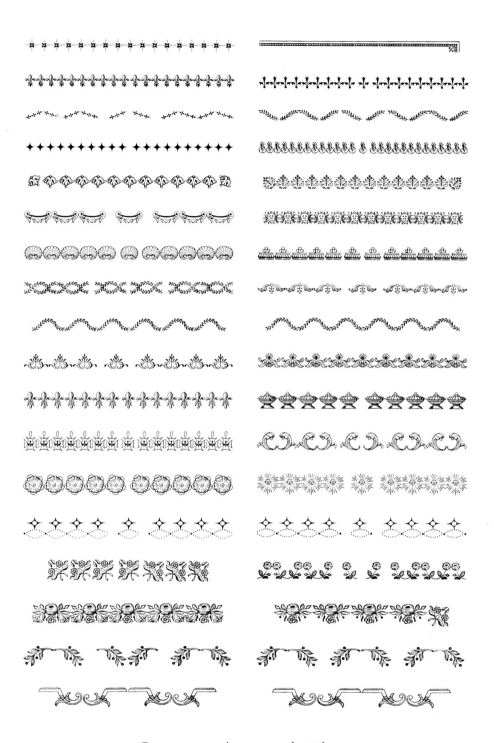

Row ornaments in rococo style, 18th cn.

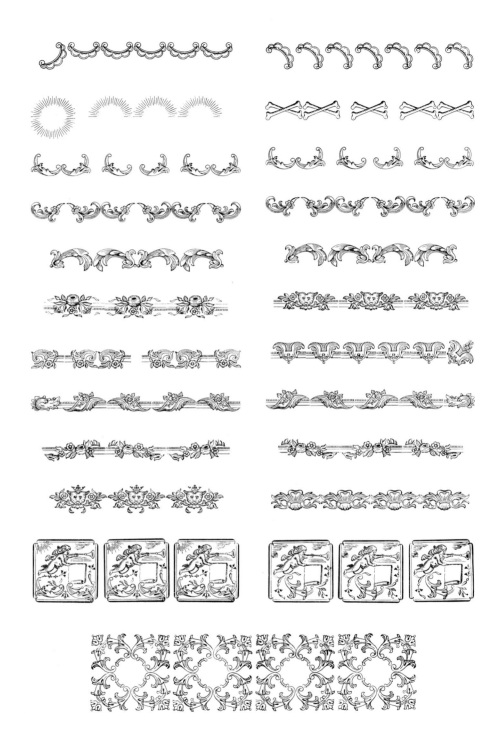

Row ornaments in rococo style, 18th cn.

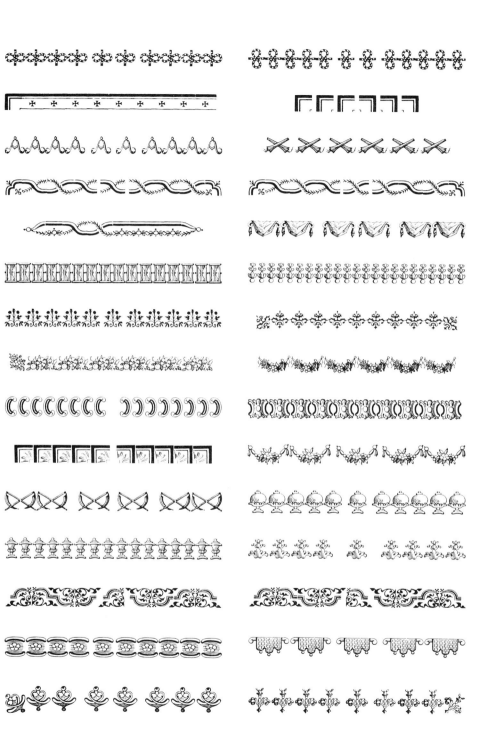

Row ornaments in rococo style, 18th cn.

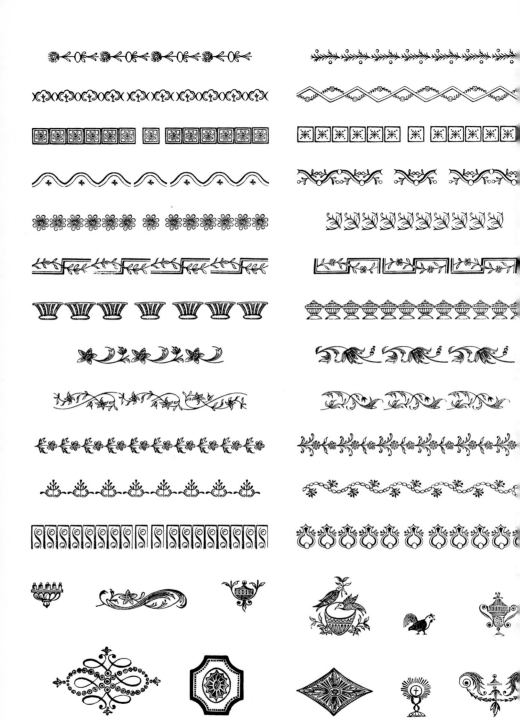

Row ornaments in rococo style, 18th cn.

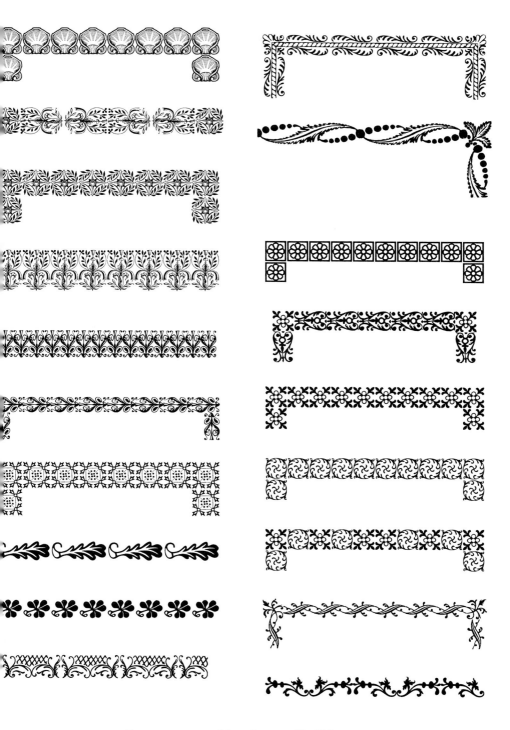

Row ornaments with various motifs, 20th cn.

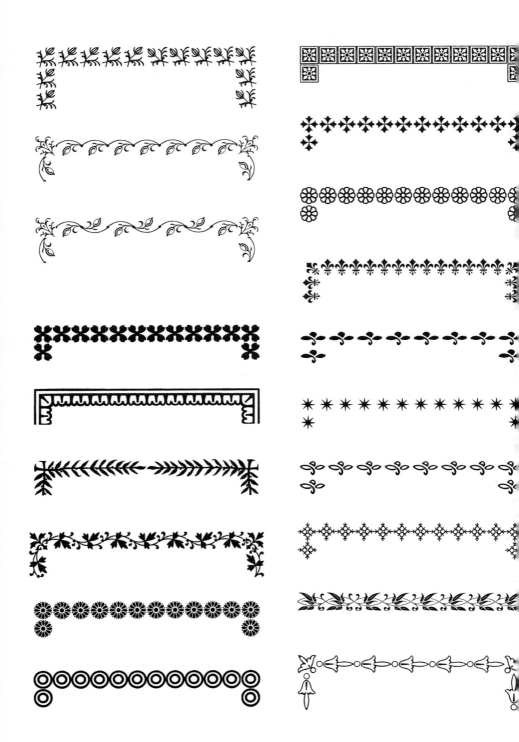

Row ornaments with various motifs, 20th cn.

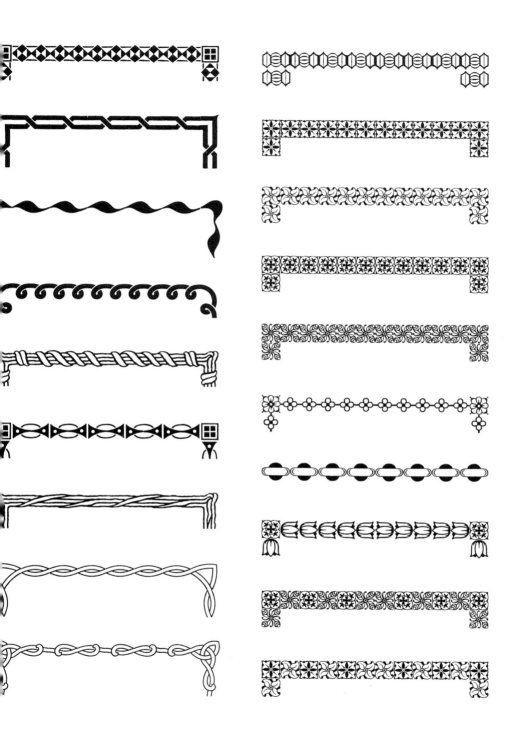

Row ornaments with various motifs, 20th cn.

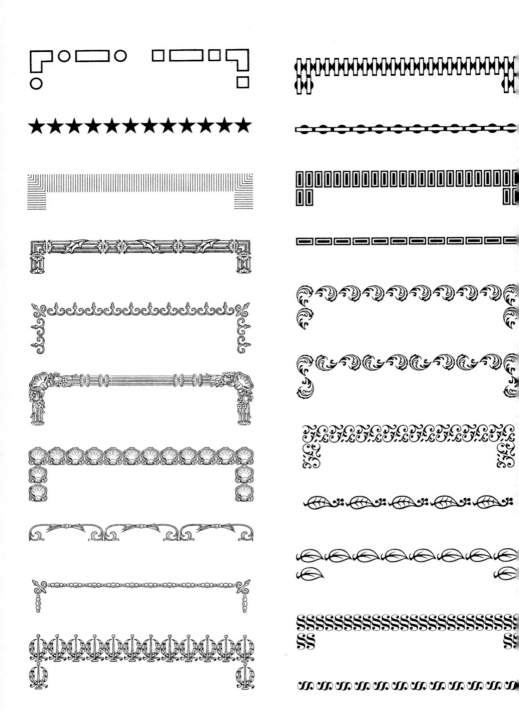

Row ornaments with various motifs, 20th cn.

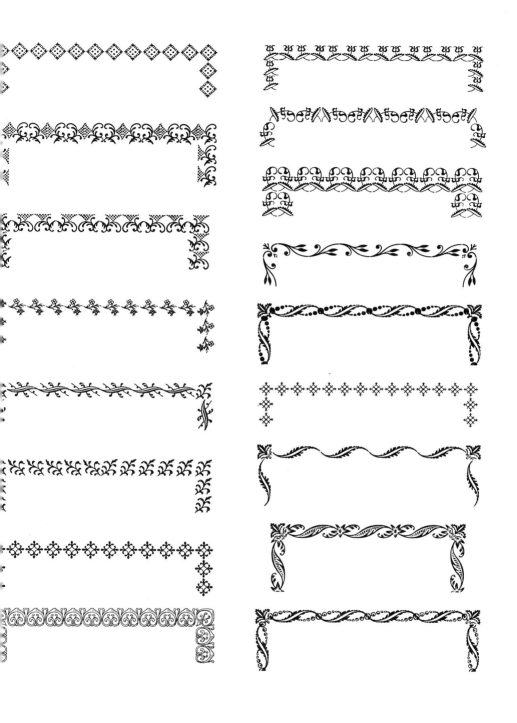

Row ornaments with various motifs, 20th cn.

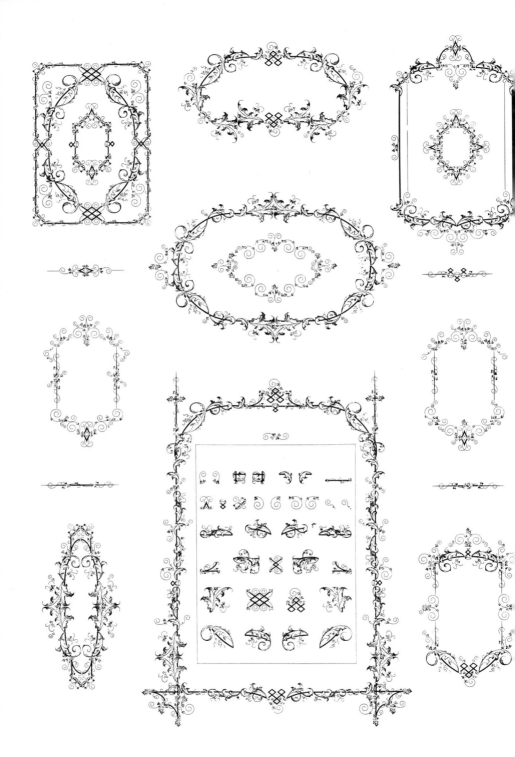

Row ornaments in rococo style. Academicism, 19th cn.

Row ornaments in rococo style. Academicism, 19th cn.

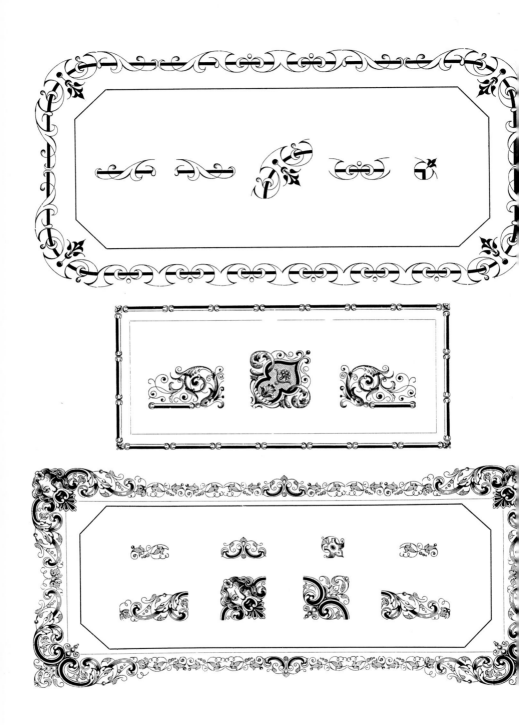

Row ornaments in rococo style. Academicism, 19th cn.

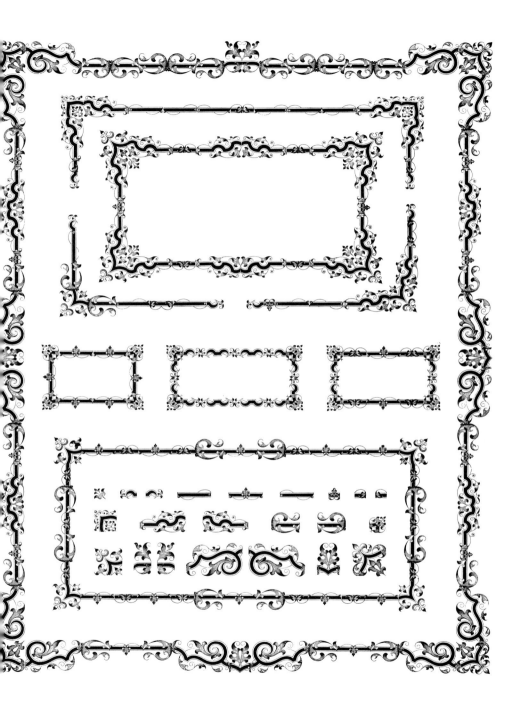

Row ornaments with arabesque motifs. Academicism, 19th cn.

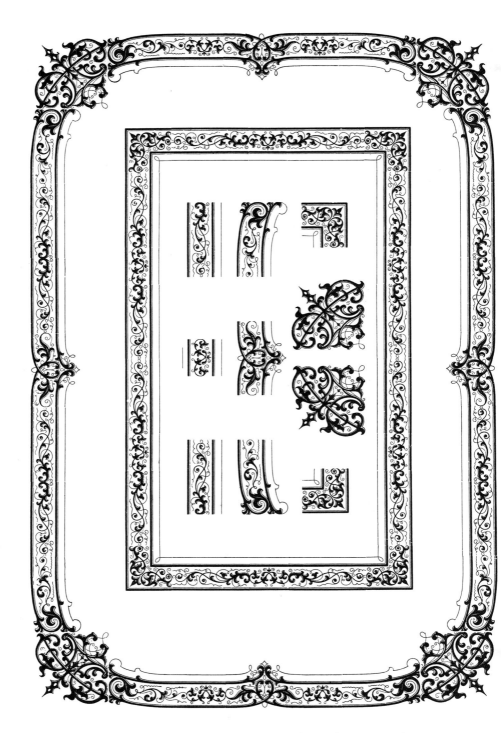

Row ornaments with arabesque motifs. Academicism, 19th cn.

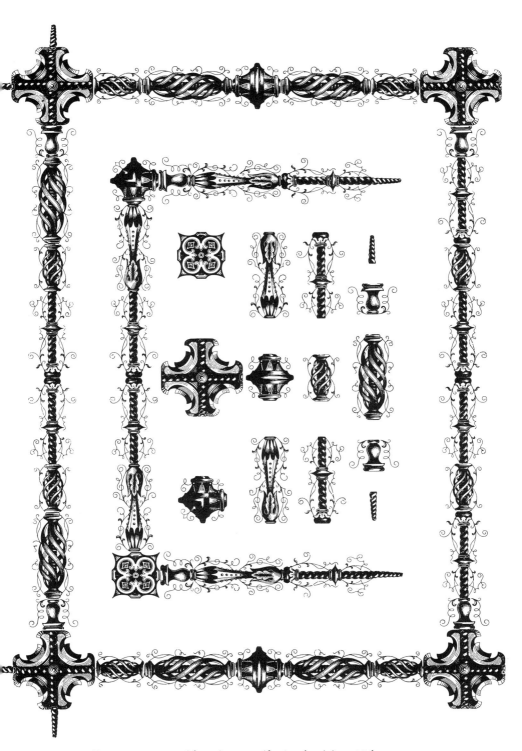

Row ornaments with various motifs. Academicism, 19th cn.

Row ornaments with various stylistic elements. Academicism, 19th cn.

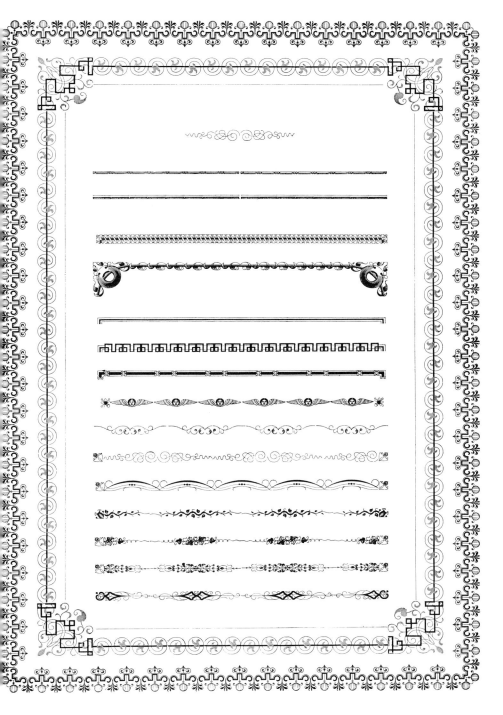

Row ornaments with various stylistic elements. Academicism, 19th cn.

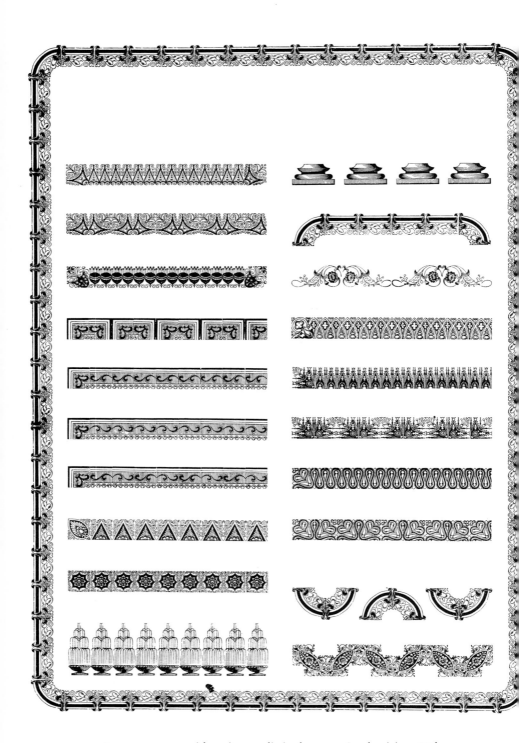

Row ornaments with various stylistic elements. Academicism, 19th cn.

Row ornaments with various stylistic elements. Academicism, 19th cn.

Row ornaments with various stylistic elements. Academicism, 19th cn.

Row ornaments with various stylistic elements. Academicism, 19th cn.

Row ornaments with various stylistic elements. Academicism, 19th cn.

Row ornaments with various stylistic elements. Academicism, 19th cn.

Row ornaments with classic style elements, 1839

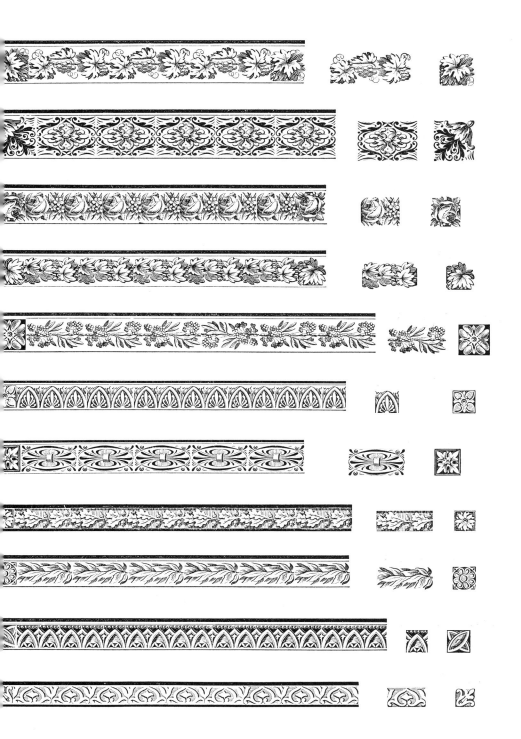

Row ornaments with classic style elements, 1839

Row ornaments with classic style elements, 1839

Row ornaments with classic style elements, 1839

Row ornaments with classic style elements, 1839

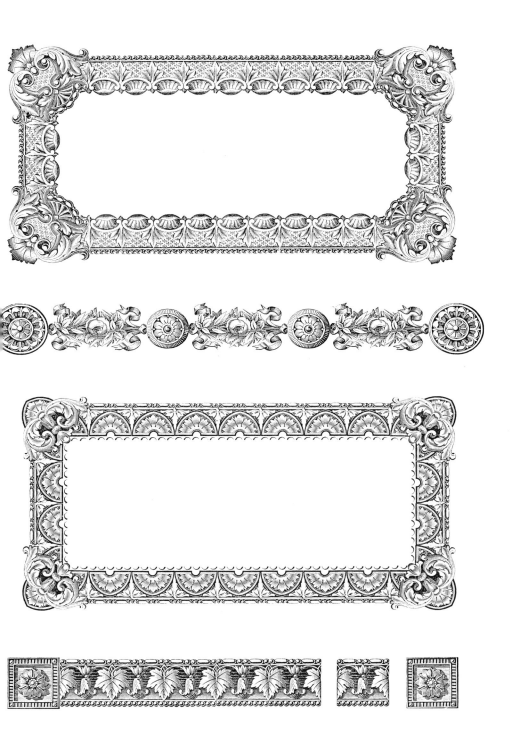

Row ornaments with classic style elements, 1839

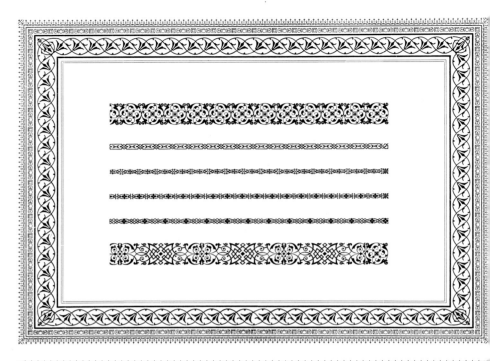

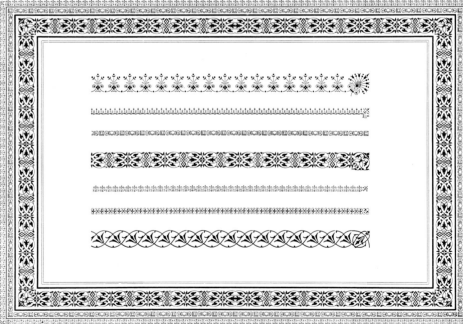

Row ornaments with various motifs, 19th cn.

Row ornaments with various motifs, 19th cn.

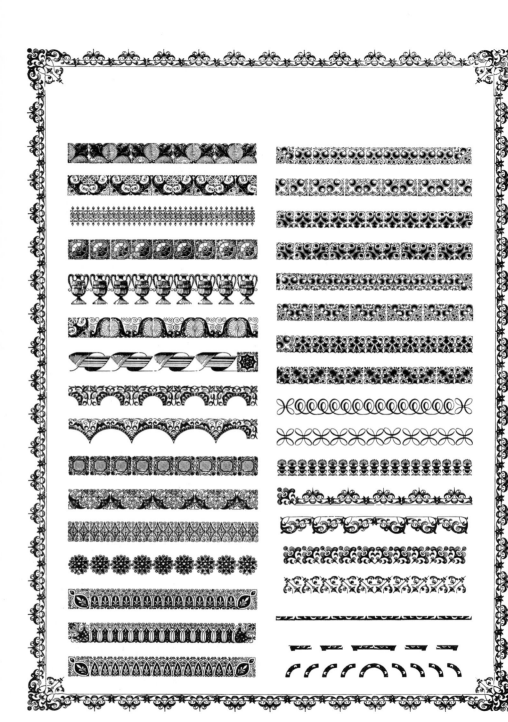

Row ornaments with various motifs, 19th cn.

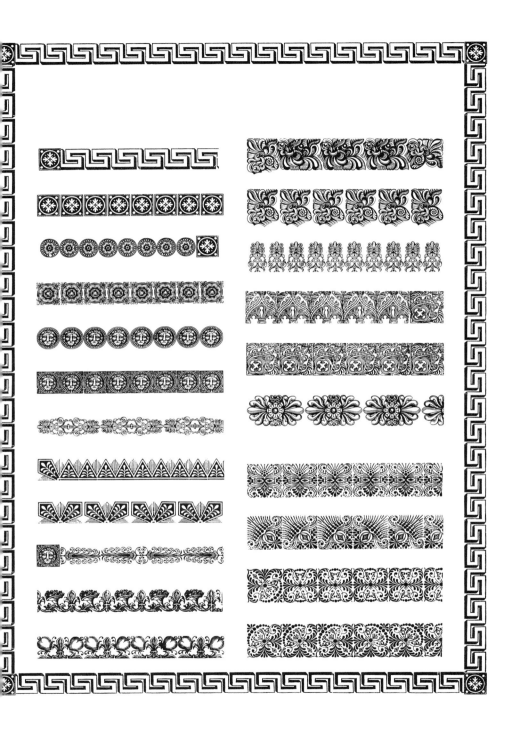

Row ornaments with various motifs, 19th cn.

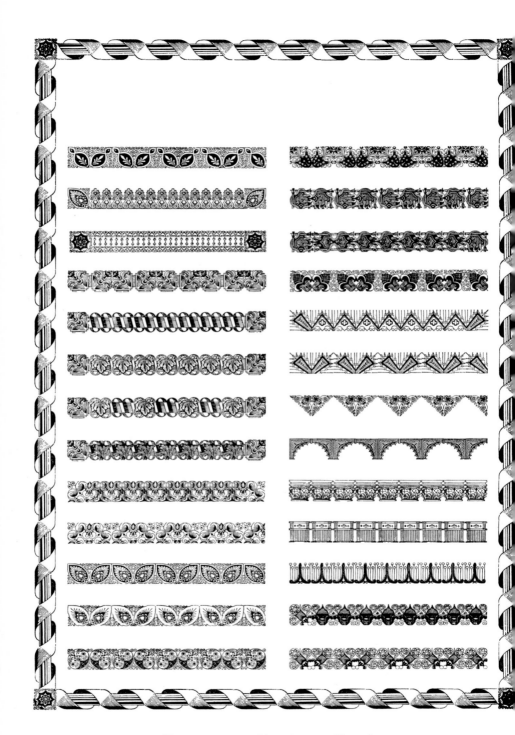

Row ornaments with various motifs, 19th cn.

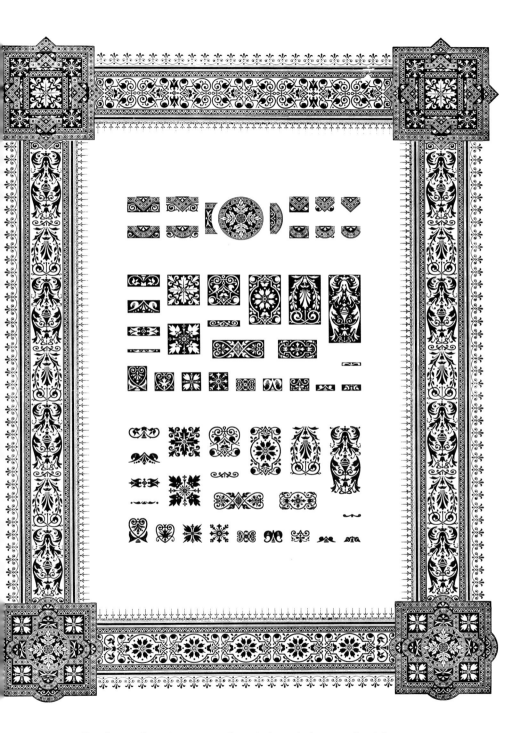

Borders and row ornament pieces in intarsia form, early 20th cn.

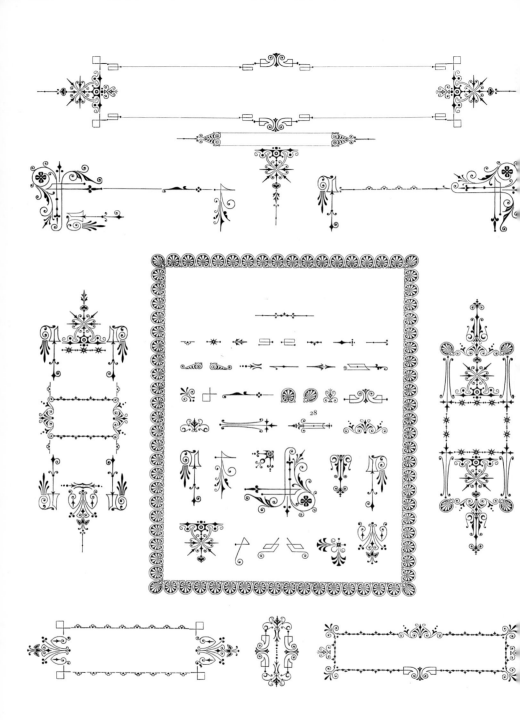

Row ornaments with various stylistic elements, 19th cn.

Row ornaments with Art Nouveau motifs, early 20th cn.

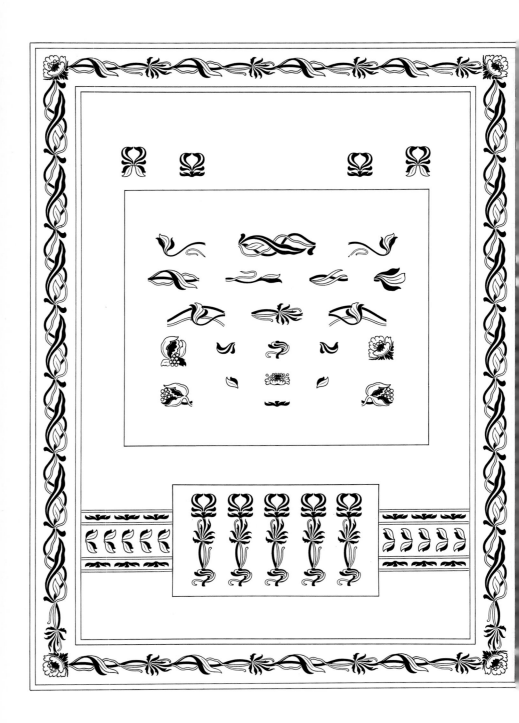

Row ornaments with Art Nouveau motifs, early 20th cn.

Row ornaments with Art Nouveau motifs, early 20th cn.

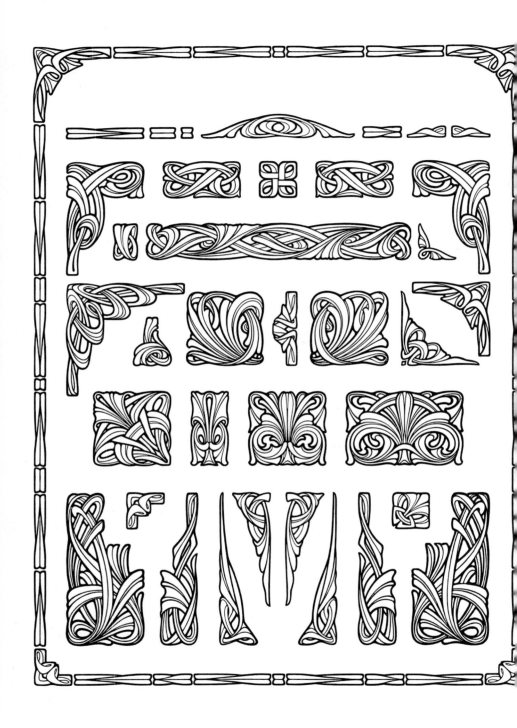

Row ornaments with Art Nouveau motifs, early 20th cn.

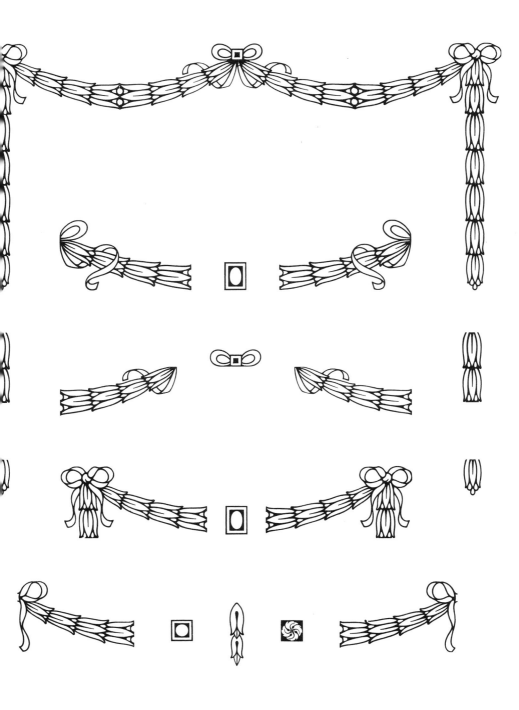

Row ornaments with Art Nouveau motifs, early 20th cn.

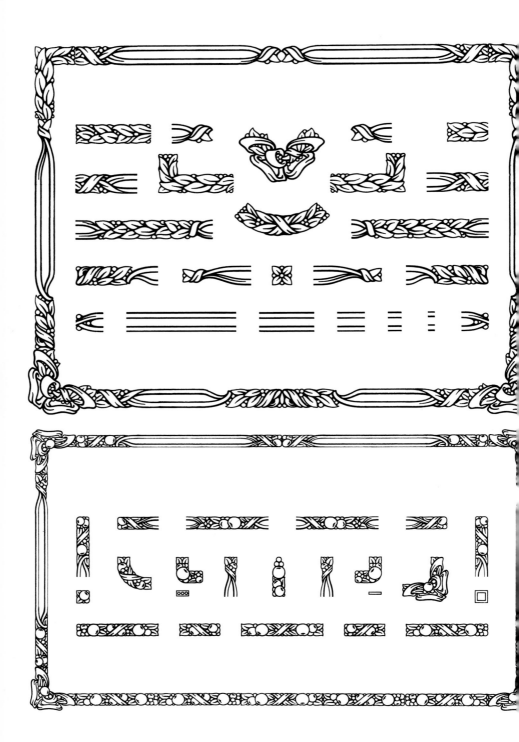

Row ornaments with Art Nouveau motifs, early 20th cn.

Row ornaments with Art Nouveau motifs, early 20th cn.

Row ornaments with Art Nouveau motifs, early 20th cn.

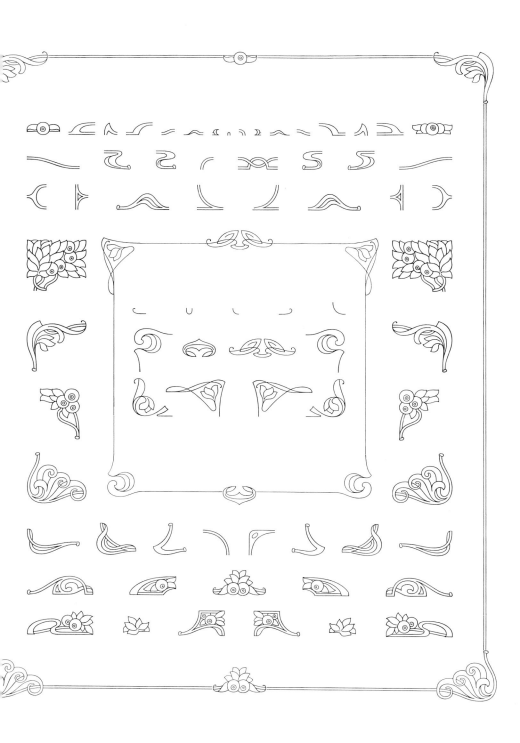

Row ornaments with Art Nouveau motifs, early 20th cn.

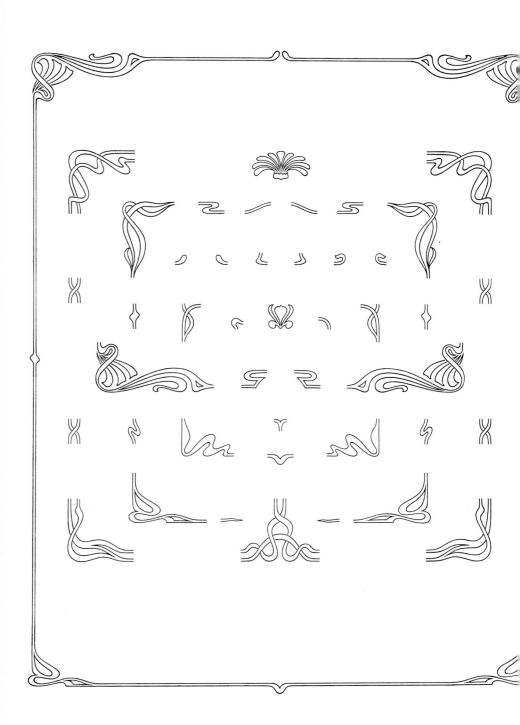

Row ornaments with Art Nouveau motifs, early 20th cn.

Row ornaments with Art Nouveau motifs, early 20th cn.

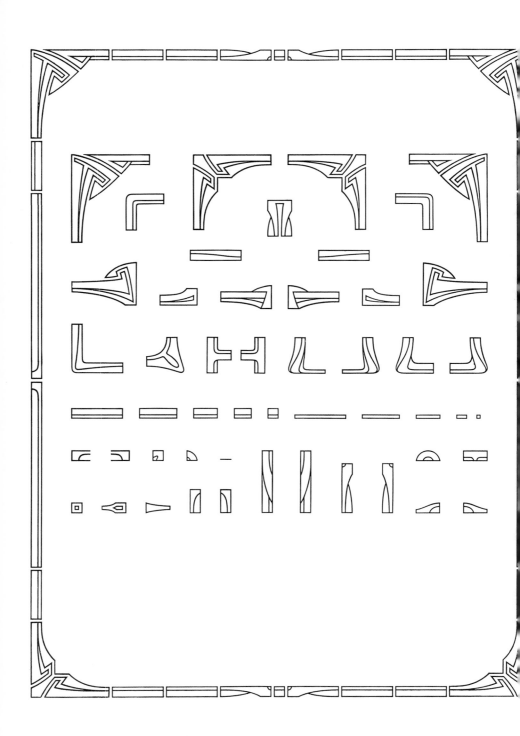

Row ornaments with Art Nouveau motifs, early 20th cn.

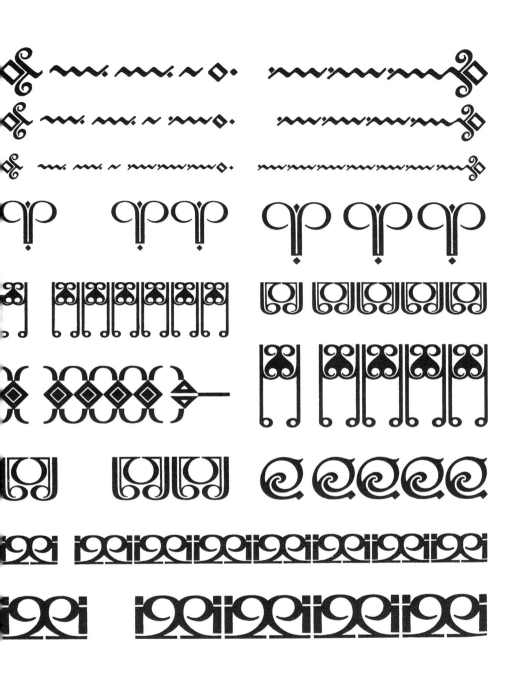

Decorative row ornaments. Peter Behrens, 1908

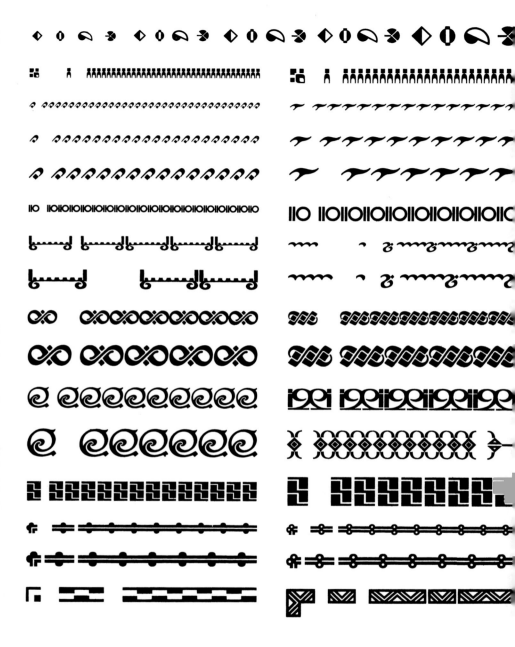

Decorative row ornaments. Peter Behrens, 1908

Decorative row ornaments and corner-pieces. Peter Behrens, 1908

Decorative row ornaments and corner-pieces. Peter Behrens, 1908

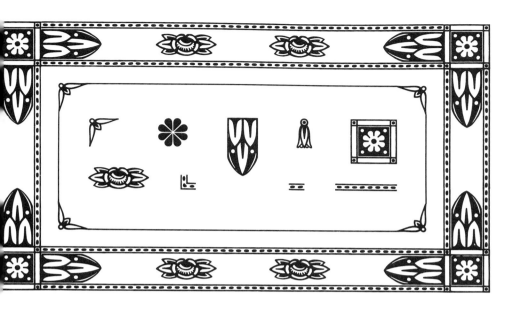

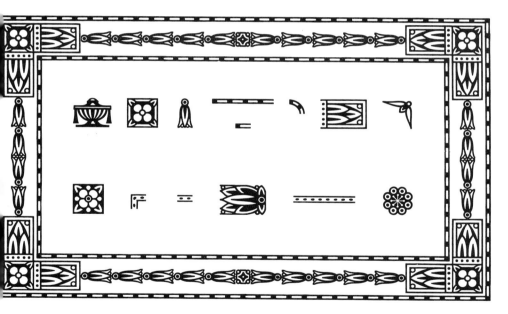

Decorative row ornaments. Art Nouveau, about 1910

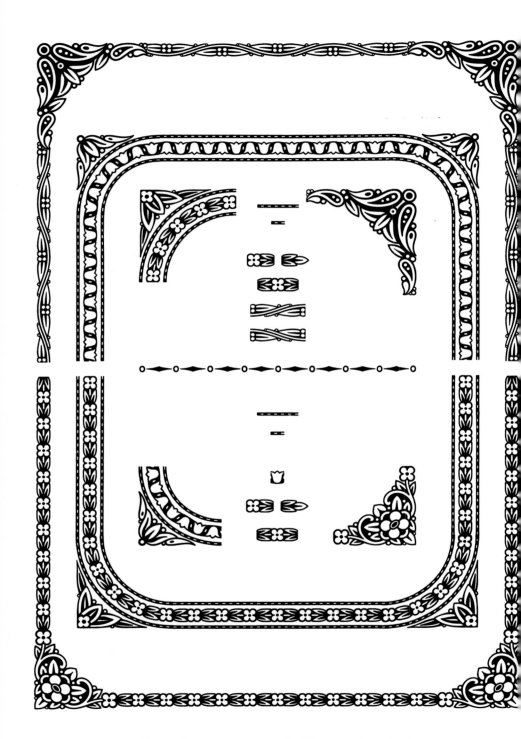

Decorative row ornaments. Art Nouveau, about 1910

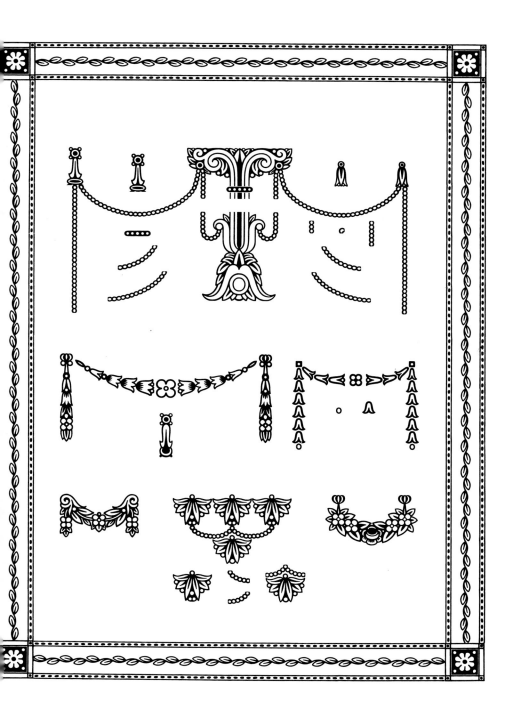

Decorative row ornaments. Art Nouveau, about 1910

239

Decorative row ornaments. Art Nouveau, about 1910

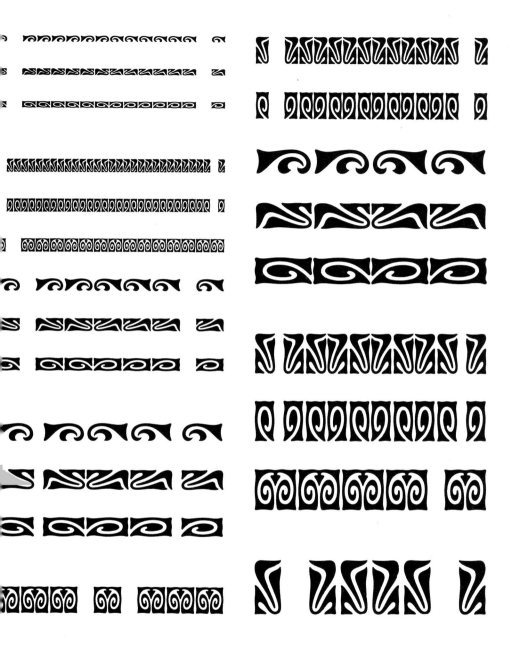

Decorative row ornaments. Art Nouveau, about 1910

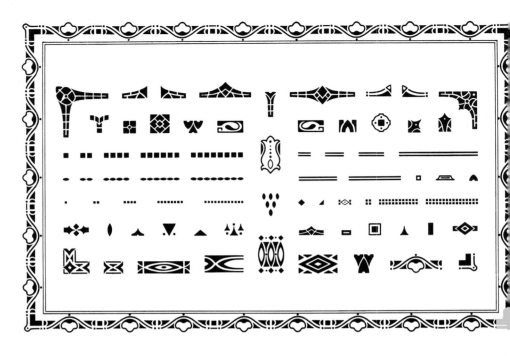

Decorative row ornaments. Art Nouveau, about 1910

Decorative row ornaments. Art Nouveau, about 1910

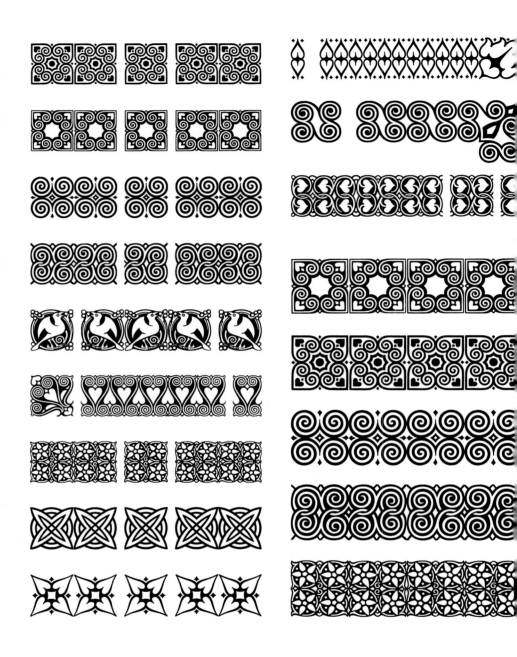

Borders. Friedrich Wilhelm Kleukens, about 1910

Borders. Heinz Keune, about 1910

Row ornaments with lotus leaf motifs, about 1911

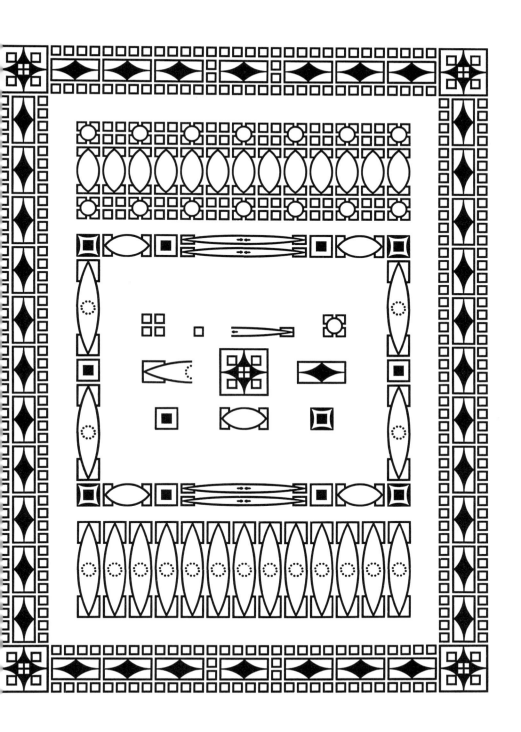

Row ornaments, Art Nouveau, about 1911

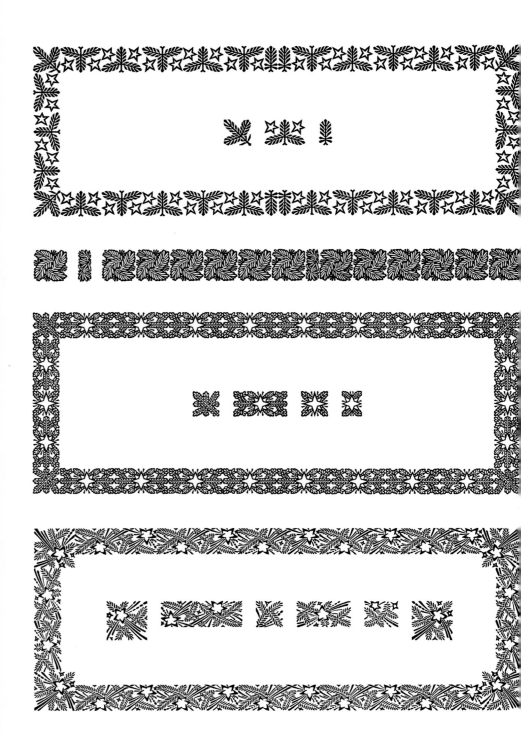

Christmas decorations, 20th cn.

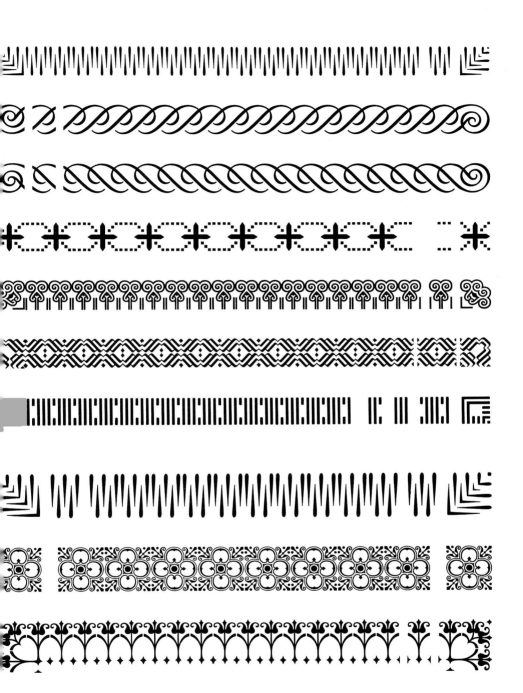

Row ornaments. Wieynk, early 20th cn.

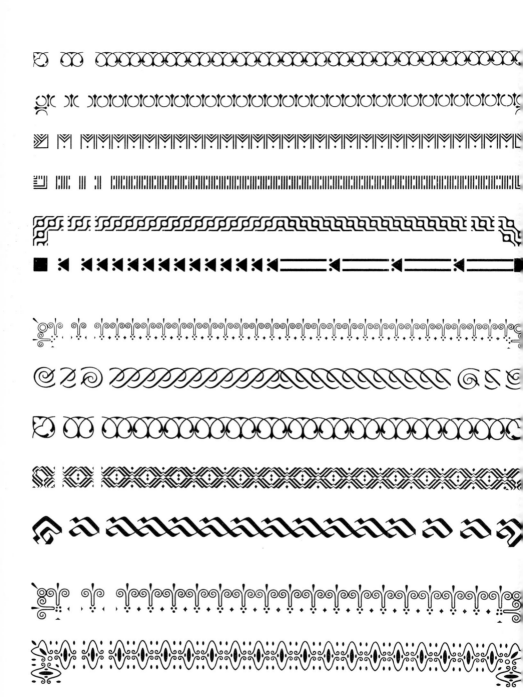

Row ornaments. Wieynk, early 20th cn.

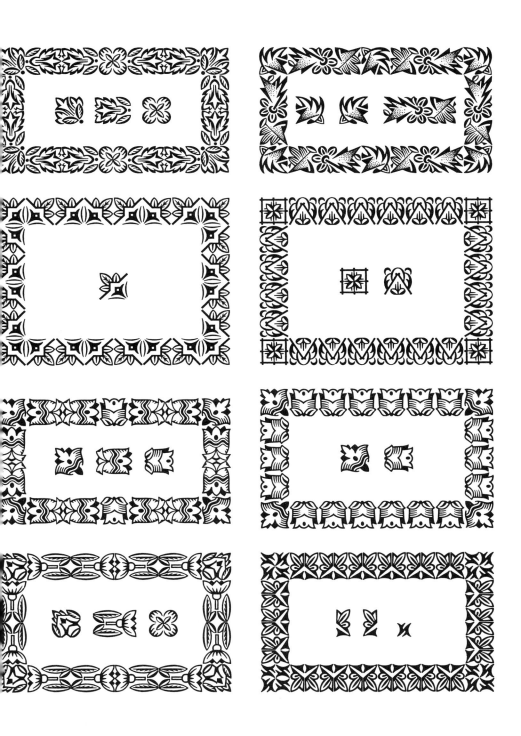

Row ornaments, Art Nouveau

Row ornaments, Art Nouveau

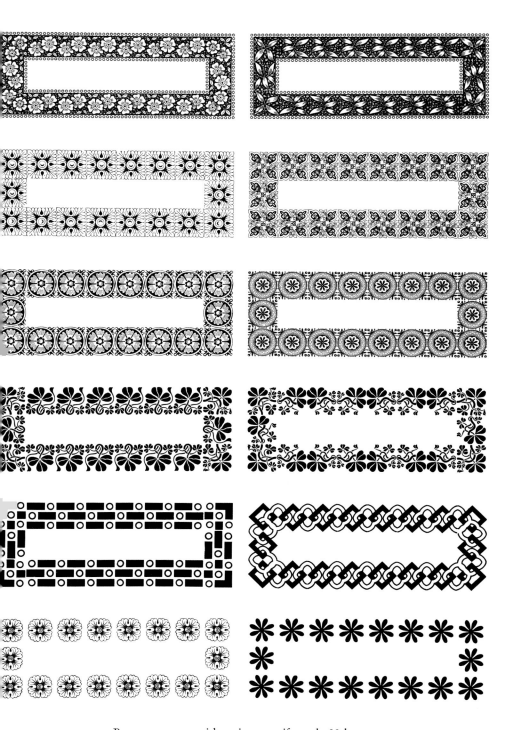

Row ornaments with various motifs, early 20th cn.

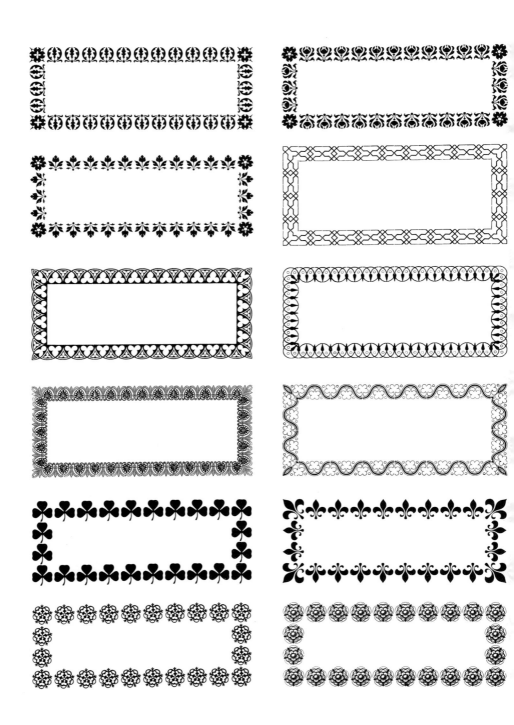

Row ornaments with various motifs, early 20th cn.

Row ornaments with various motifs, early 20th cn.

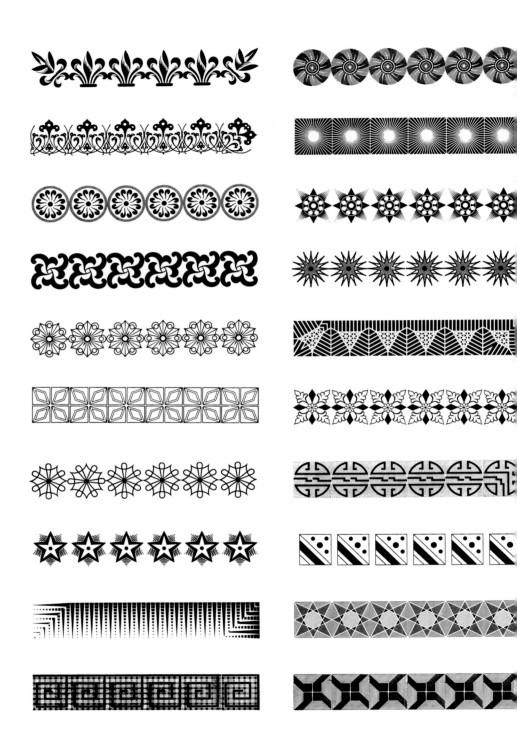

Row ornaments with various motifs, early 20th cn.

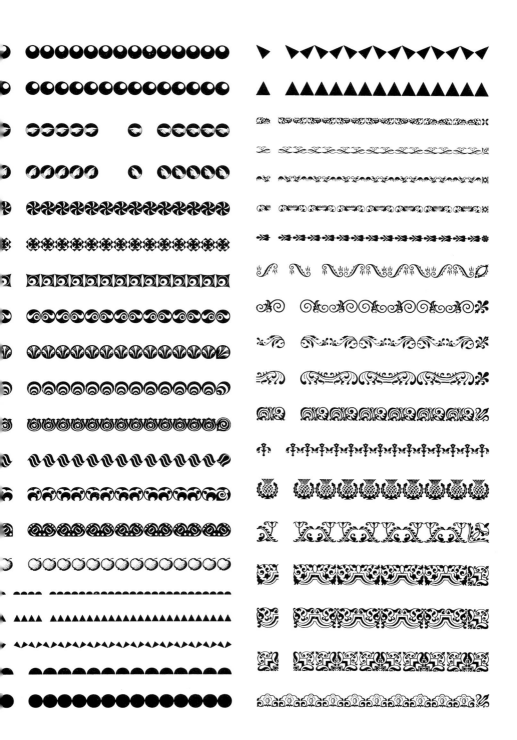

Row ornaments with various stylistic elements, 20th cn.

257

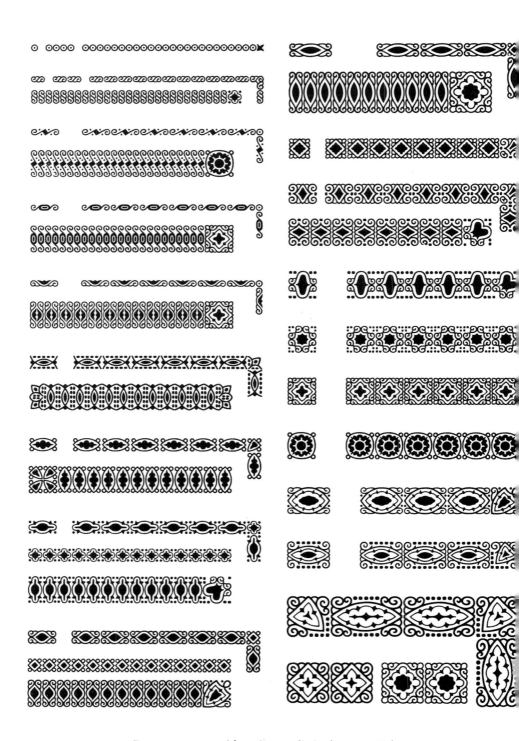

Row ornaments with various stylistic elements, 20th cn.

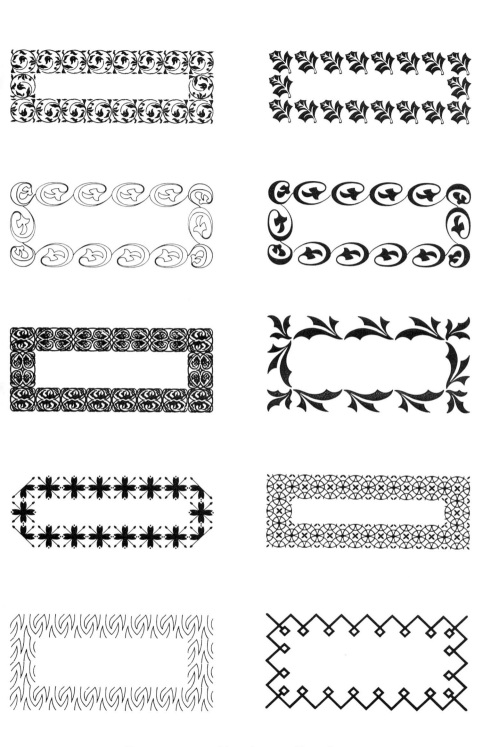

Row ornaments with various motifs, 20th cn.

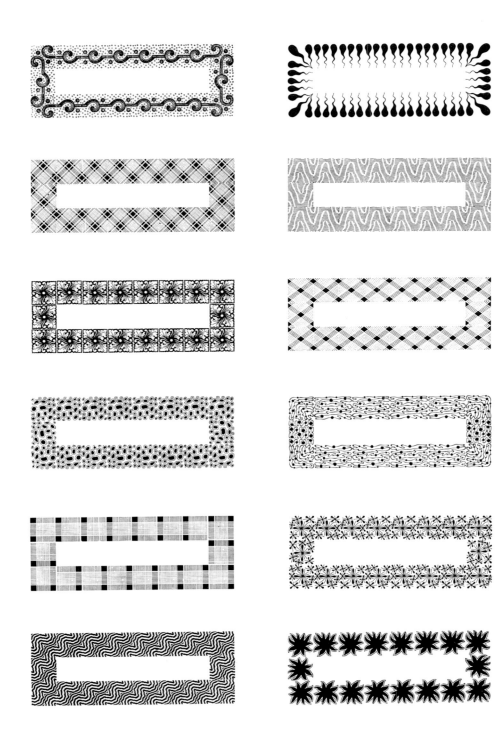

Row ornaments with various motifs, 20th cn.

Row ornaments with various motifs, 20th cn.

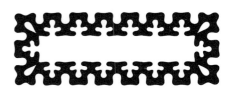
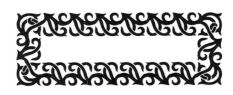

Row ornaments with various motifs, 20th cn.

Row ornaments with various motifs, 20th cn.

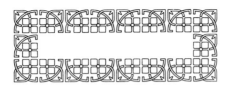
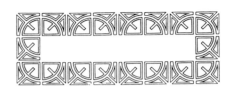

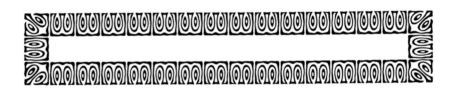

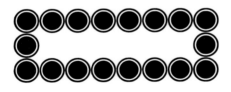

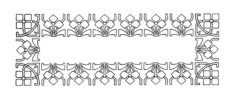
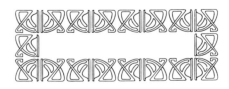

Row ornaments with various motifs, 20th cn.

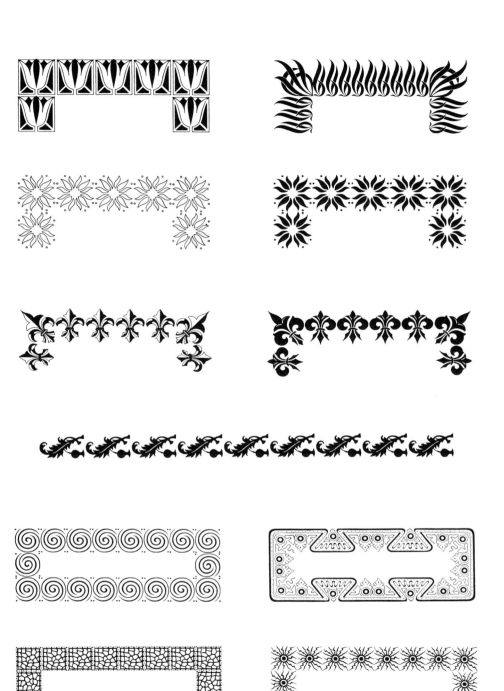

Row ornaments with various motifs, 20th cn.

Row ornaments with various motifs, 20th cn.

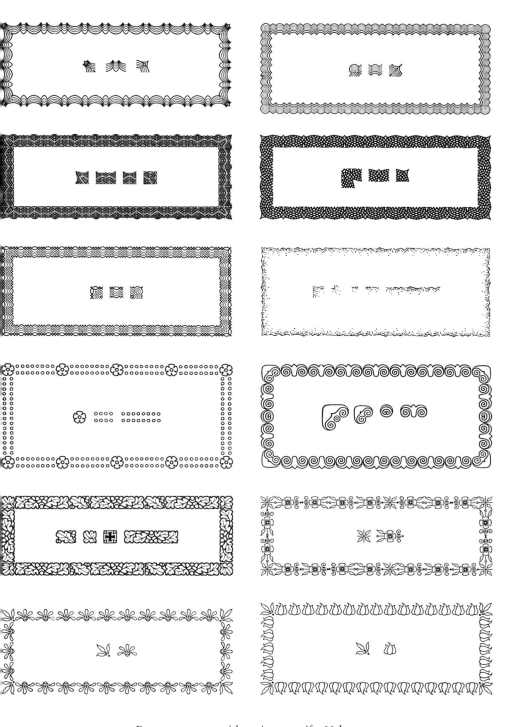

Row ornaments with various motifs, 20th cn.

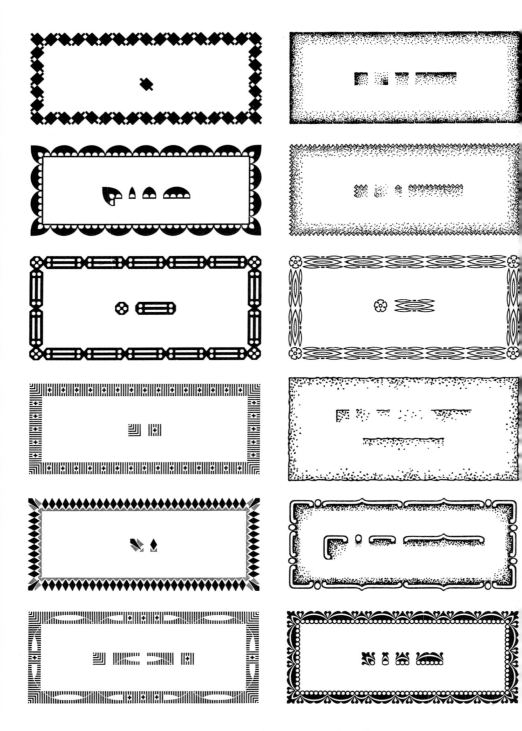

Row ornaments with various motifs, 20th cn.

Row ornaments with various motifs, 20th cn.

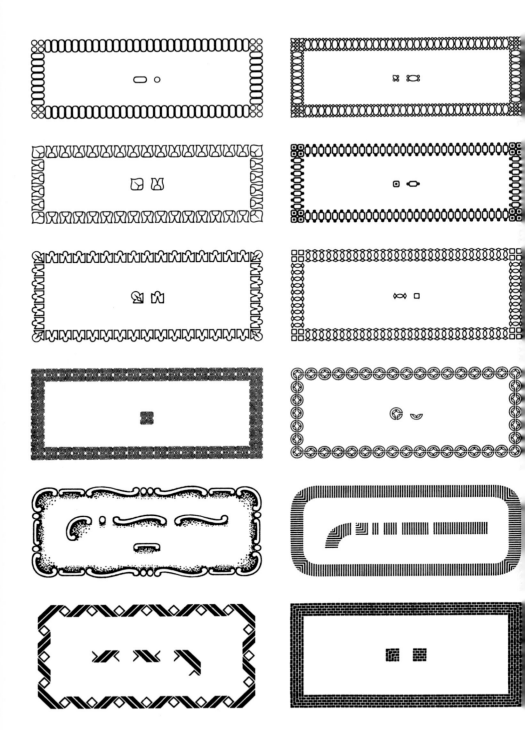

Row ornaments with various motifs, 20th cn.

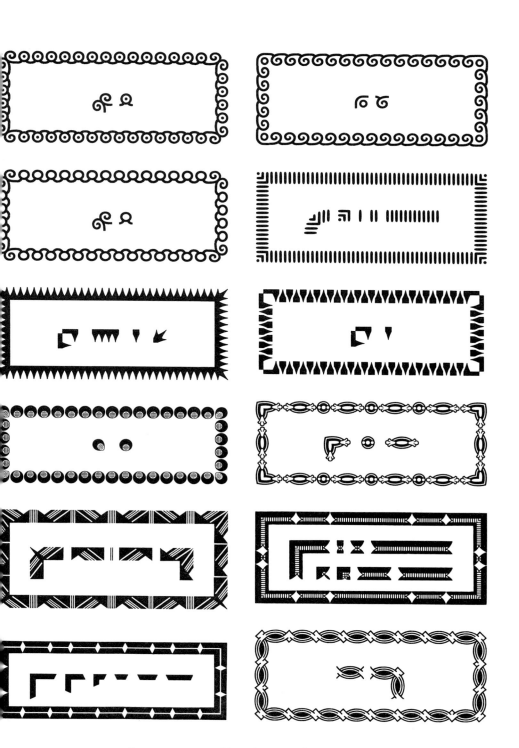

Row ornaments with various motifs, 20th cn.

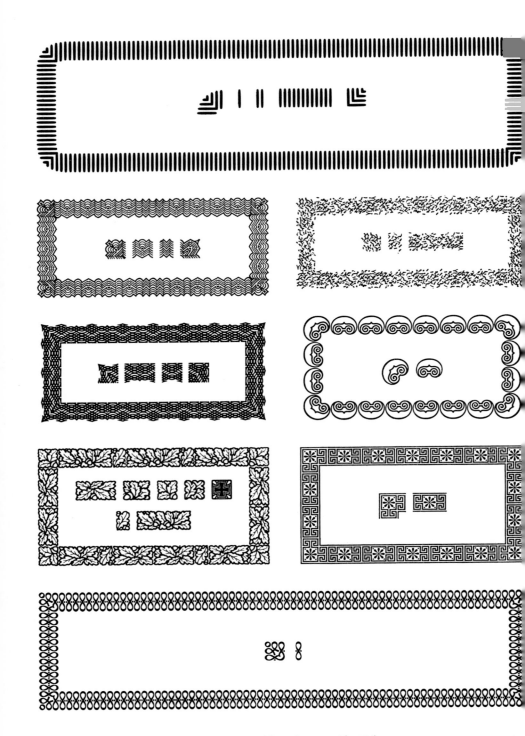

Row ornaments with various motifs, 20th cn.

Row ornaments with various motifs, 20th cn.

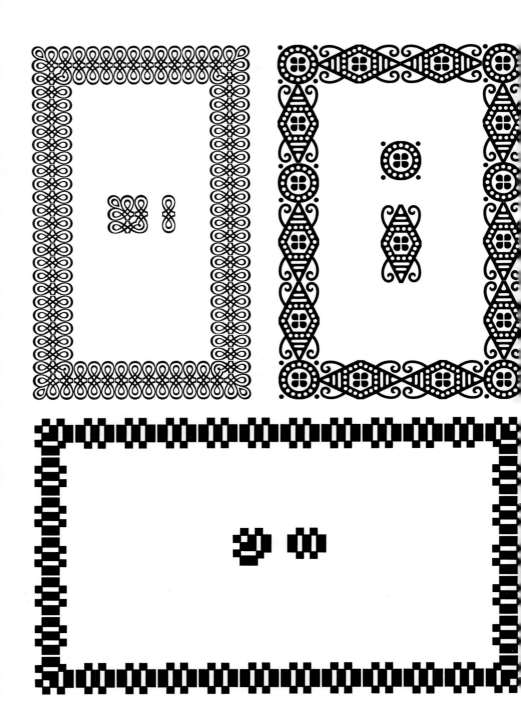

Row ornaments with various motifs, 20th cn.

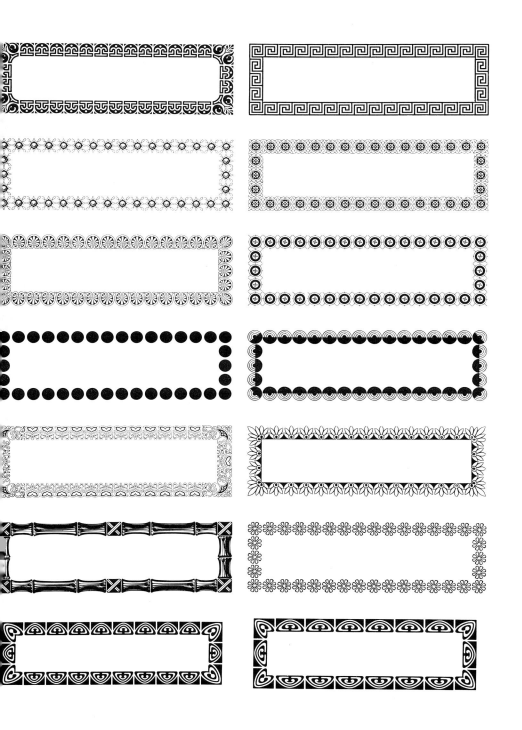

Row ornaments with various motifs, 20th cn.

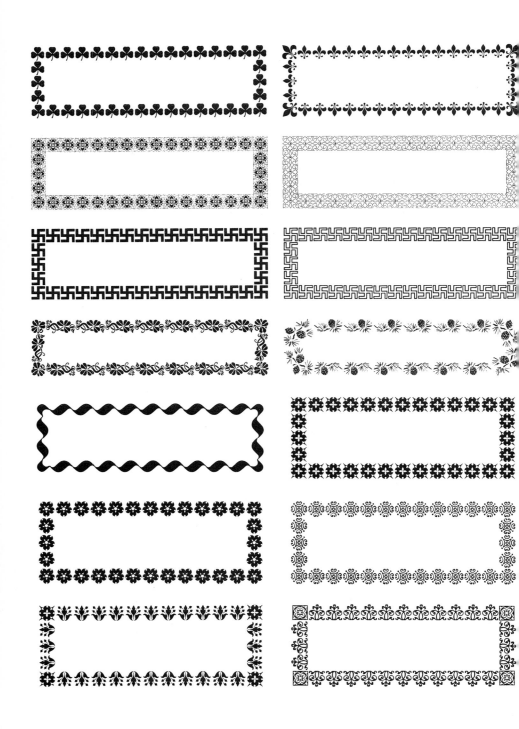

Row ornaments with various motifs, 20th cn.

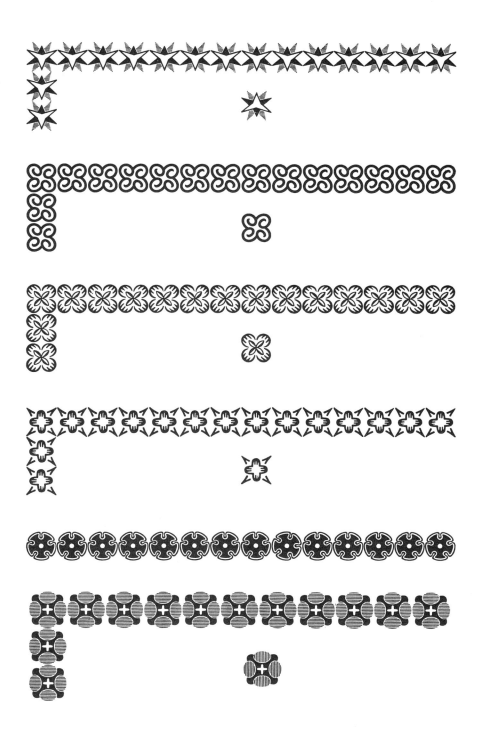

Row ornaments with various motifs, 20th cn.

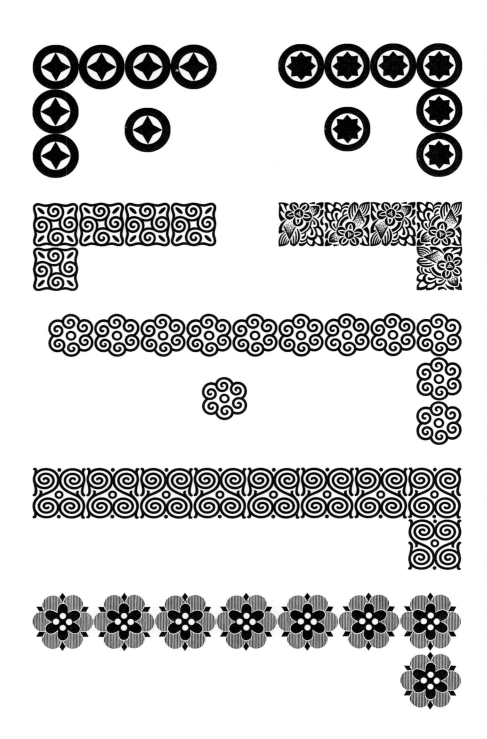

Row ornaments with various motifs, 20th cn.

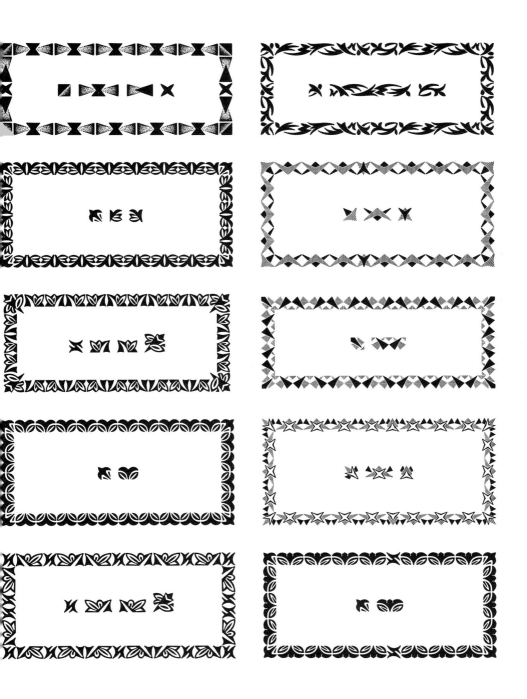

Row ornaments, Art Deco

Row ornaments, Art Deco

Row ornaments, Art Deco

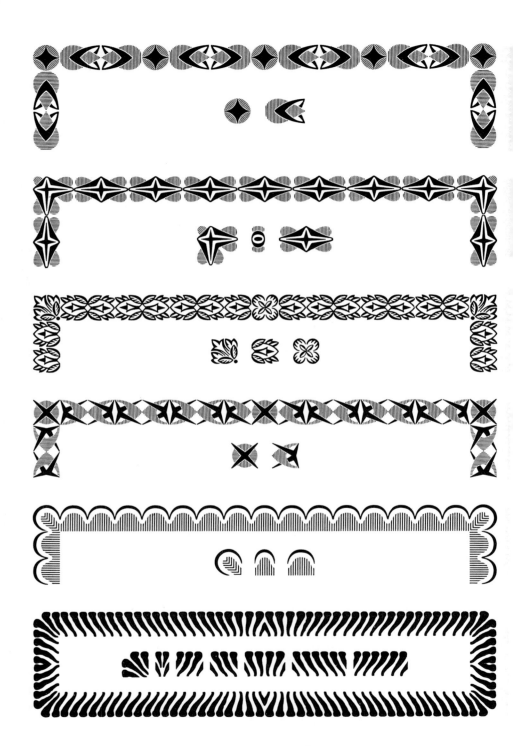

Row ornaments, Art Deco

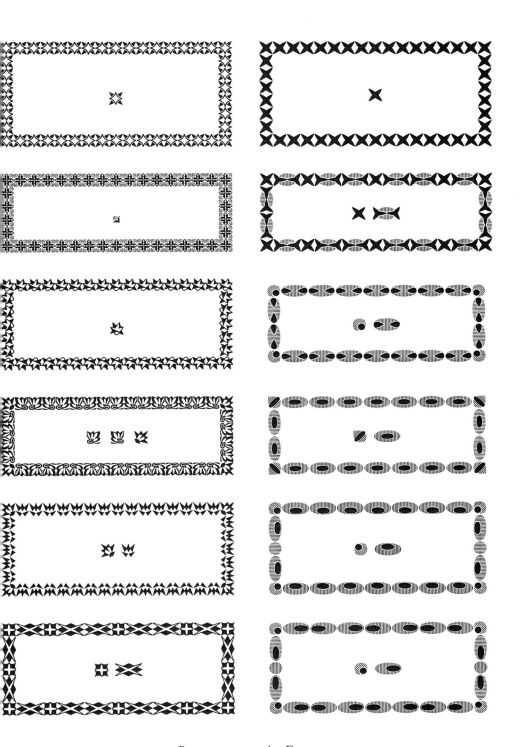

Row ornaments, Art Deco

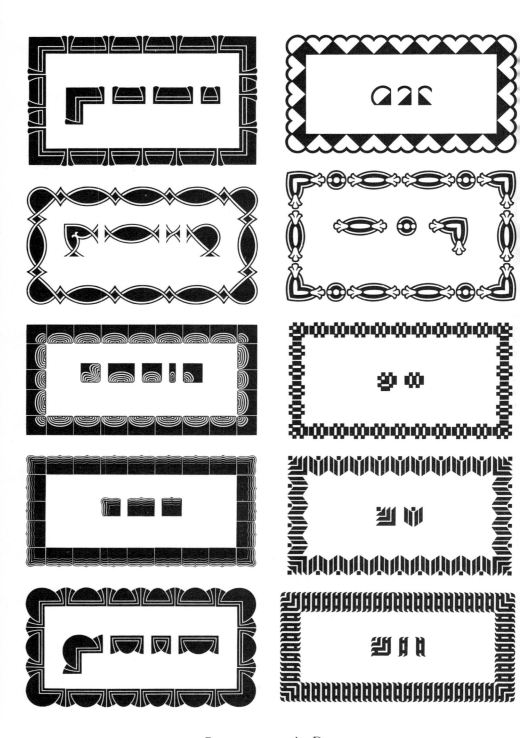

Row ornaments, Art Deco

Row ornaments, Art Deco

Row ornaments, Art Deco

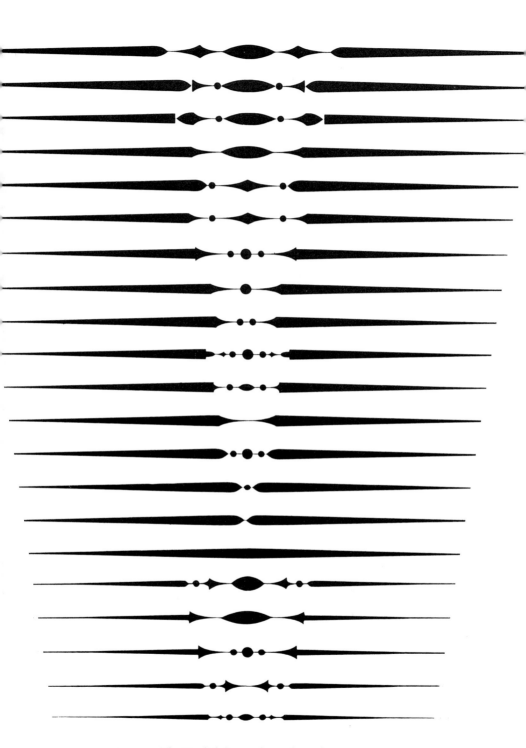

The English line, rules and panels

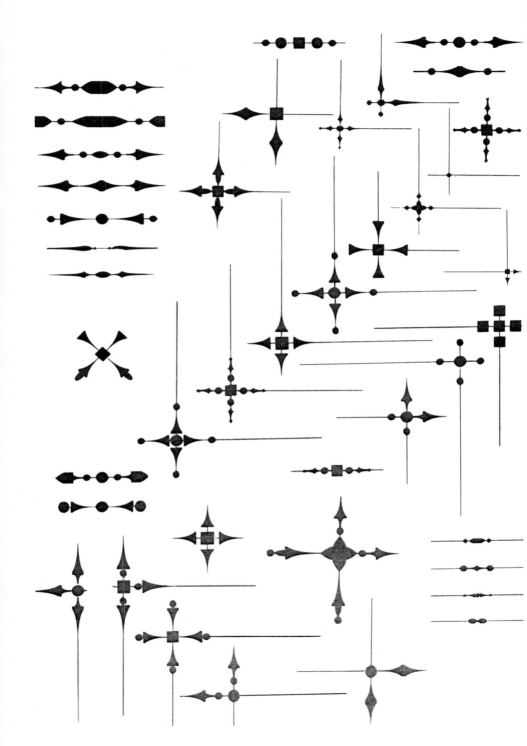

The English line, rules and panels

Ornamental areas

Basketwork. Albrecht Dürer, about 1500

Mauresque as ornamental area. Francesco Pellegrino, Paris 1530

Mauresque and strapwork. Pieter Coecke (?). Hieronymus Cock, Antwerp, middle of the 16th cn

292

Lace pattern. Hans Sibmacher, 1597

Granjon arabesque for an end paper. Adam Islip, London 1596

Leather wall covering. Italy, about 1600

Flocked wallpaper. Germany, 17th cn.

Book binding. Samuel Mearne, 1669

Book binding. Renaissance

Brocade paper, Johann Christoph Ledergerber publishers, Augsburg, about 1710

Brocade paper. Johann Michael Schwibecher. Augsburg, about 1725

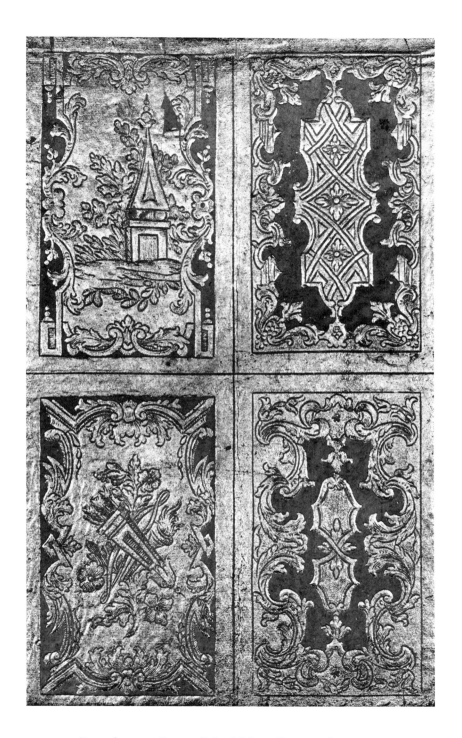

Brocade paper, Remondini publishers. Bassano, about 1760

Abdruck
von denjenigen
Röslein und Zierrathen,
welche sich
in der K. K. Hoffchriftgiefferey
bey
Johann Thomas Trattnern
dermalen befinden;

Nebft einer Probe,
wie folche fowohl
zu Anfangsbuchftaben, als
Leiften und Finalien
zufammen gefetzt werden können.

LABORE ET FAVORE.

WIEN, im Jahr 1760.

Specimen book with decorative row ornaments, ornamental areas and initials from A to Z.
Johann Thomas Trattner, Vienna 1760 (p. 302–321)

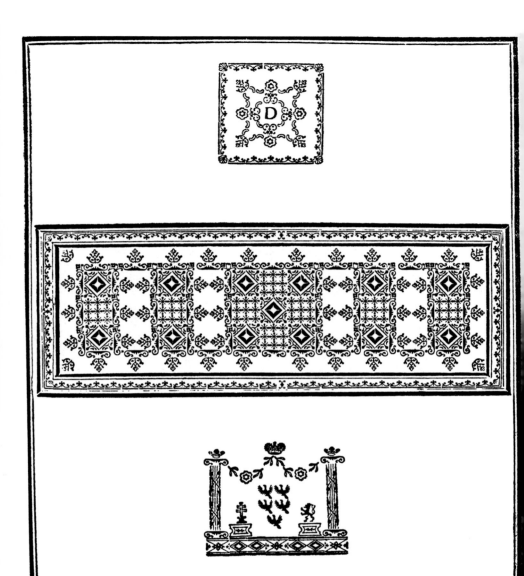

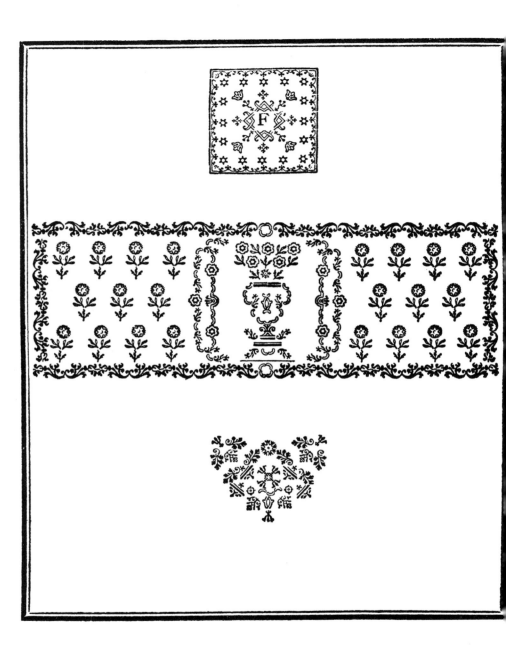

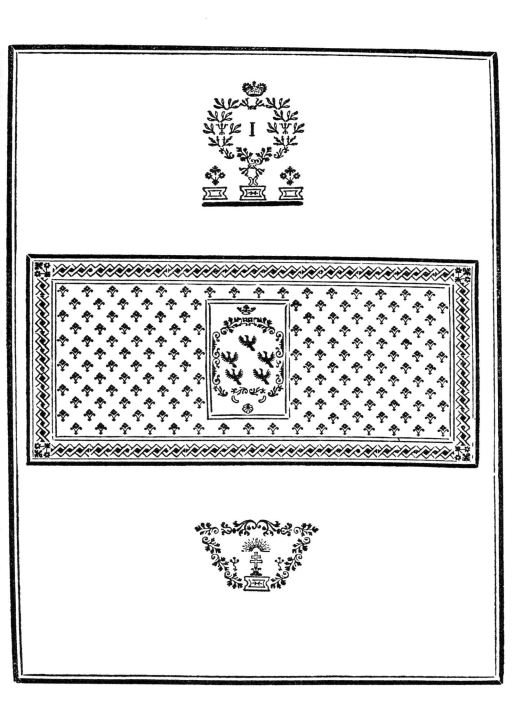

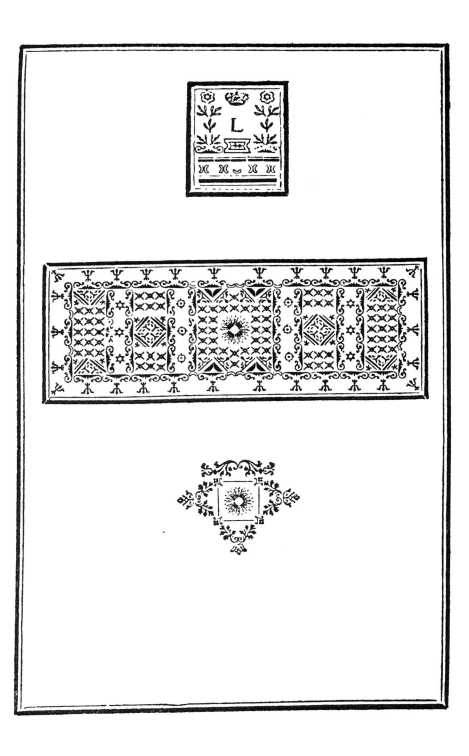

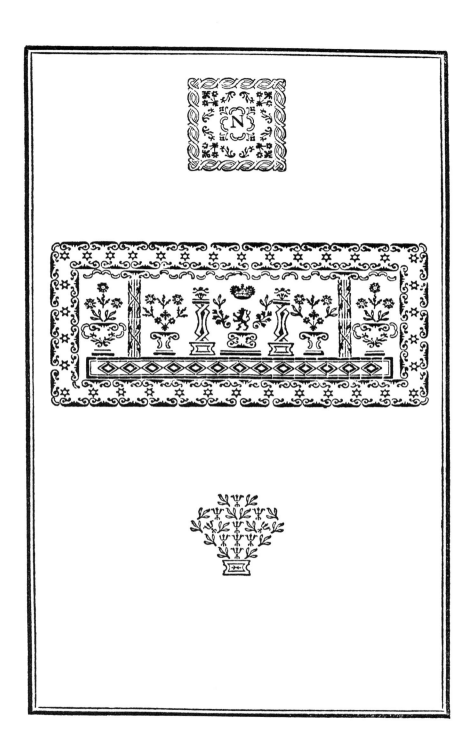

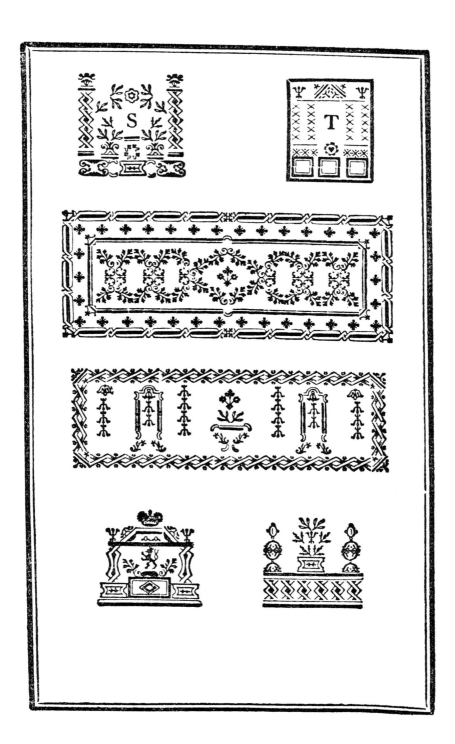

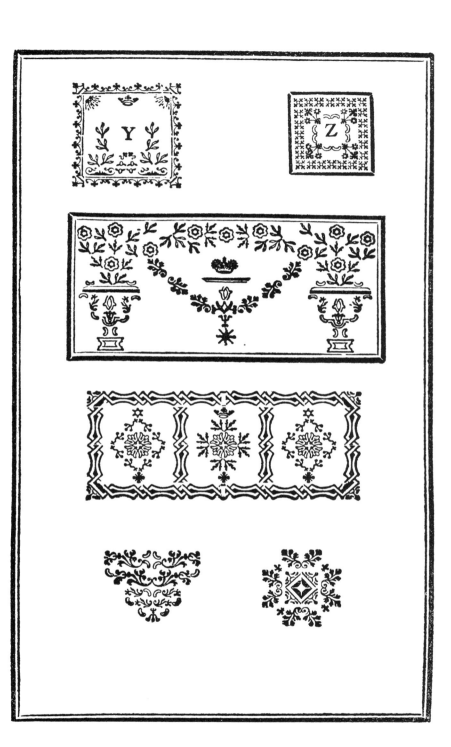

Ornamental area for background printing. Munich 1839

Ornamental area for background printing. Munich 1839

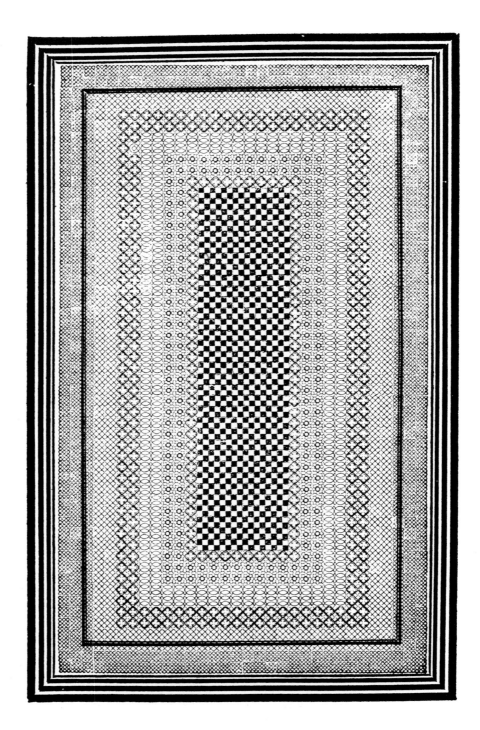

Ornamental area for background printing. Munich 1839

Ornamental area for background printing. Munich 1839

Wallpaper with Neo-Gothic design. Germany, about 1840

Wallpaper with Neo-Renaissance ornamentation. G. Bötticher, 1875

Ornamental area specimens with Neo-Renaissance motifs. Berlin 1884

Ornamental area specimens with Neo-Renaissance motifs. Berlin 1884

Wallpaper, G. L. Peine factory, Hildesheim 1966/67

Initials

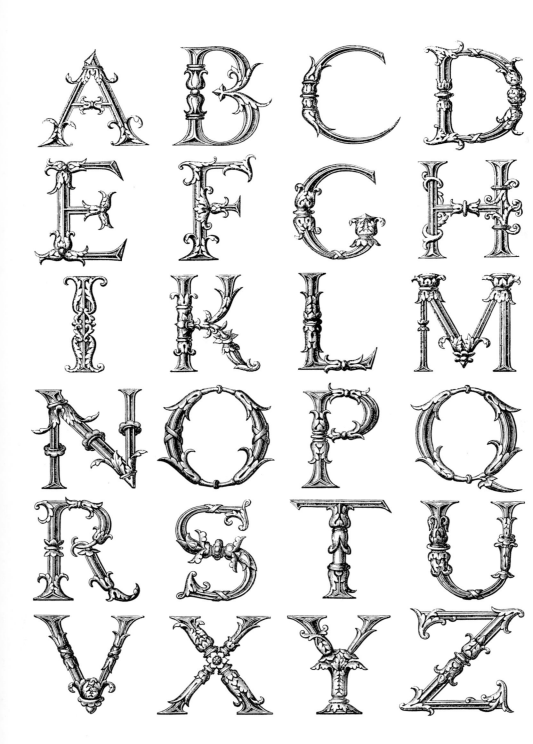

Illuminated initials, 1490

English initials from the 15th cn., London

Initials after models from the Missale Traijectense, 1515

Decorative initials from Johann Schöffer's Officin, Mainz 1518

A.

B.

D.

C.

E.

Large pen initials, Venice 1554

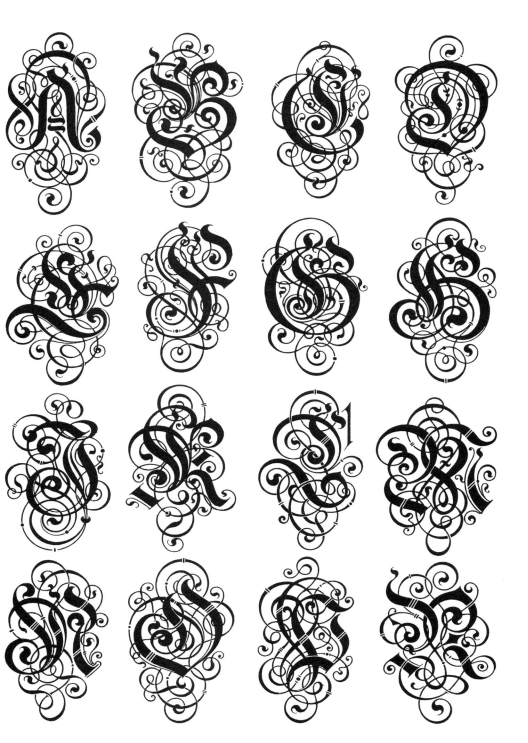

German Old-Style alphabet

Opening initials by Paulus Frank, about 1600

A.

B.

E.

F.

J.

K.

Baroque initials, 1655

Initials with tendril decorations by Oronce Finé, 1532

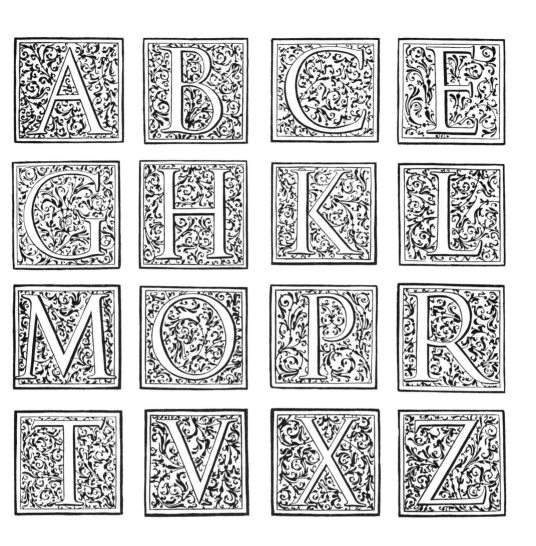

Initials with arabesques, 16th cn.

Initials, probably by Bartolomeus Voskens the elder, Amsterdam 1654

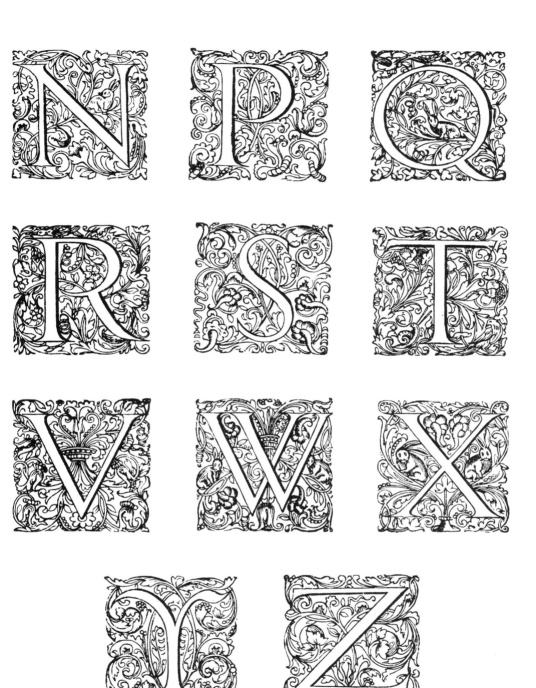

Initials, engraved by P. Versteegh, late 18th cn.

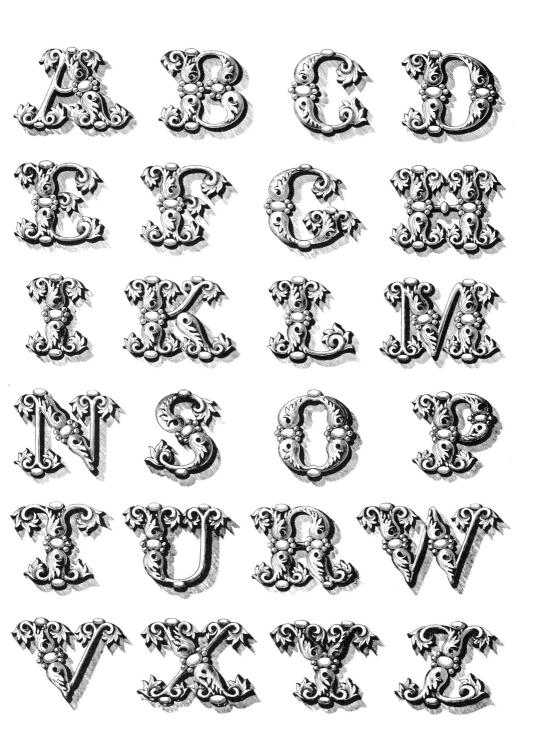

A leafy Tuscan initials design, 1845

19th cn. revival of Renaissance initials

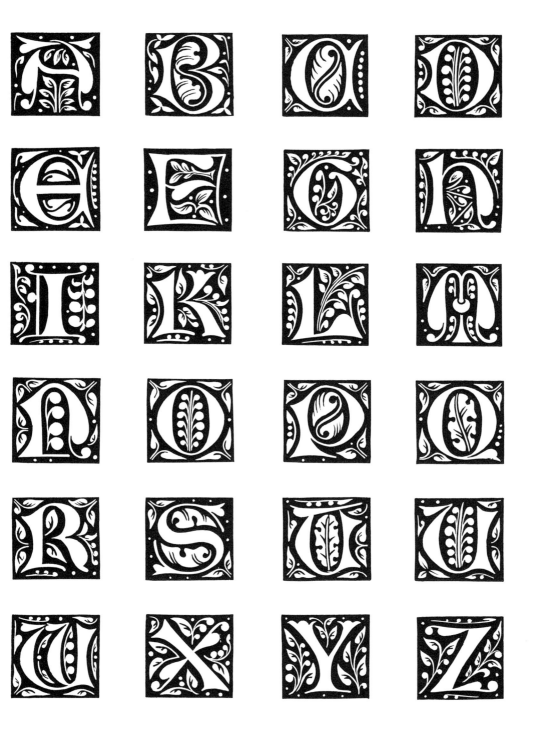

Original alphabet based on Gothic initials, middle of 19th cn.

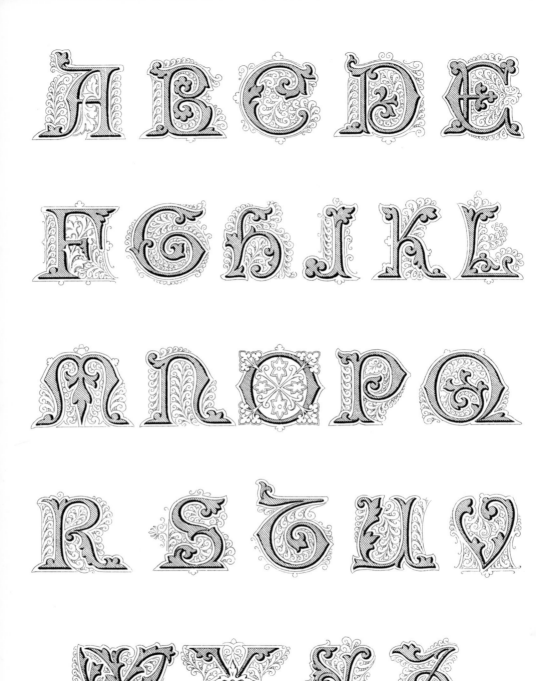

Decorative English initials

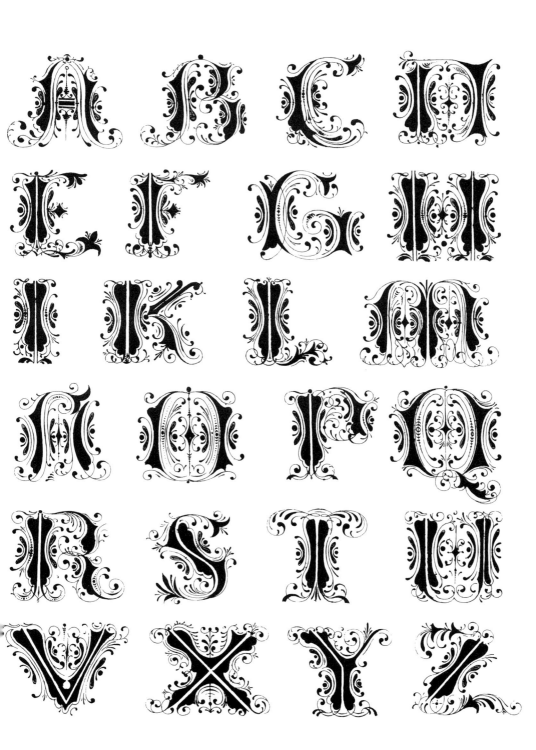

Alphabet derived from Renaissance style, 19th cn.

English initials derived from late Gothic styles, 19th cn.

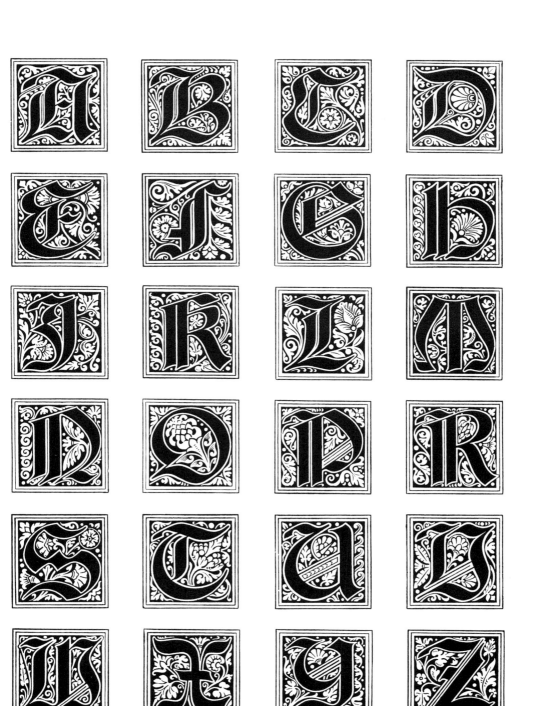

Gothic revival initials, about 1880

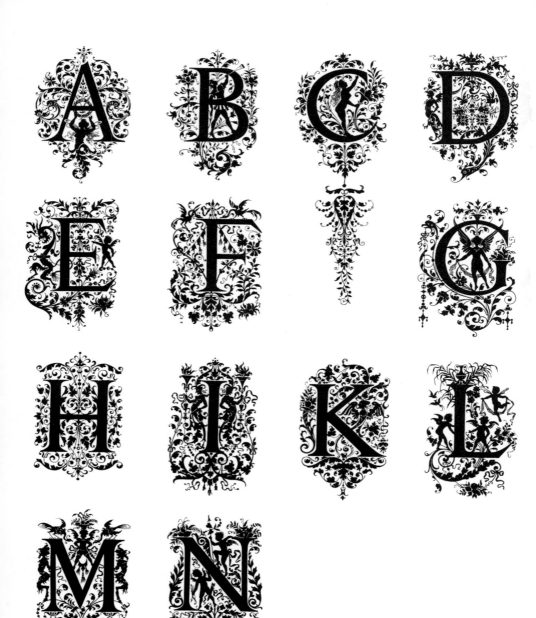

Silhouetted opening initials, 1889

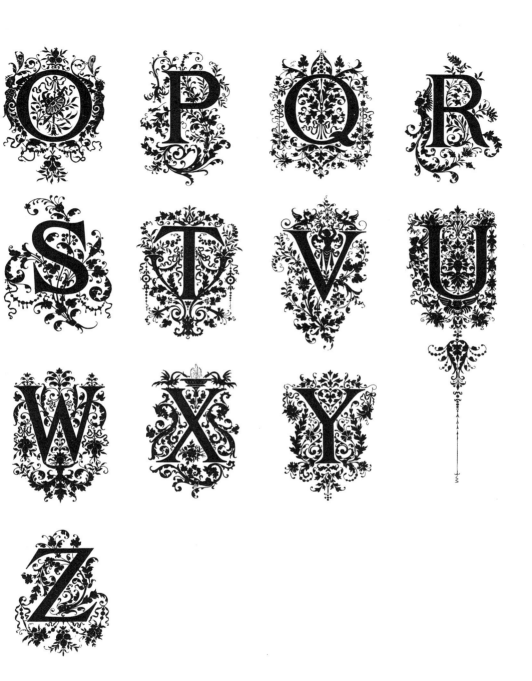

Decorative initials derived from baroque style, Berlin 1884

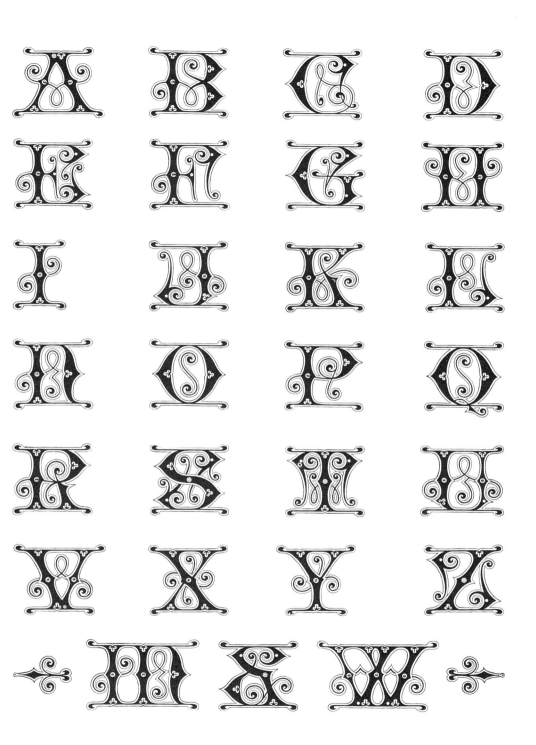

Victorian gingerbread initials, about 1890

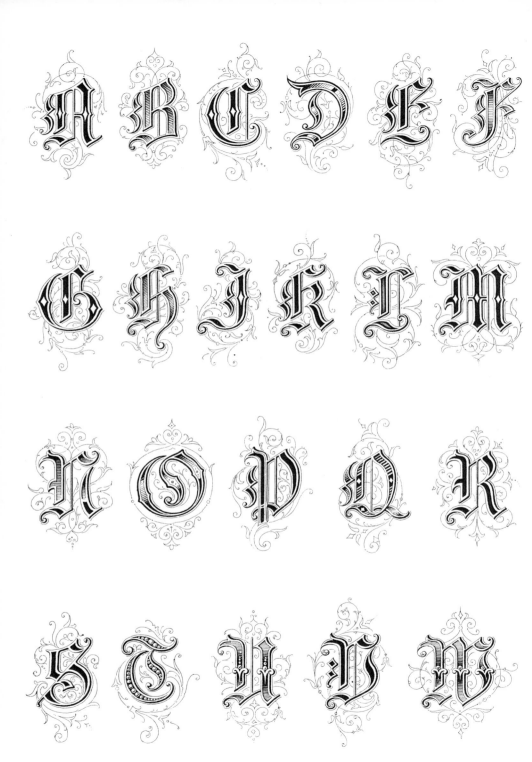

Modern black-letter initials, 19th cn.

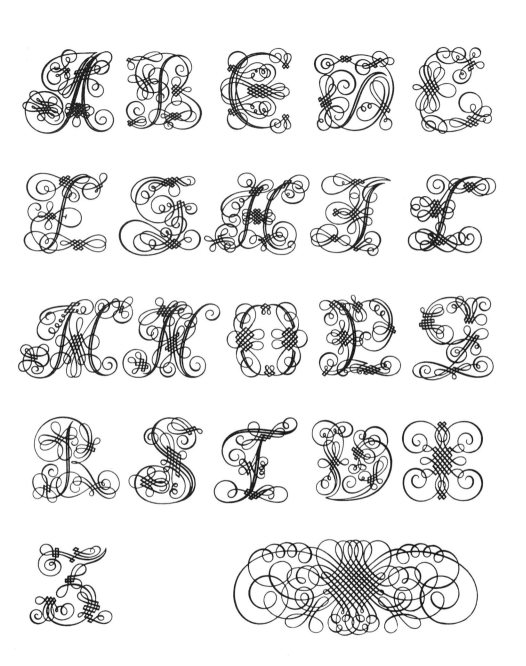

Alphabet in Renaissance manner, Andrade, Portugal, 19th cn.

357

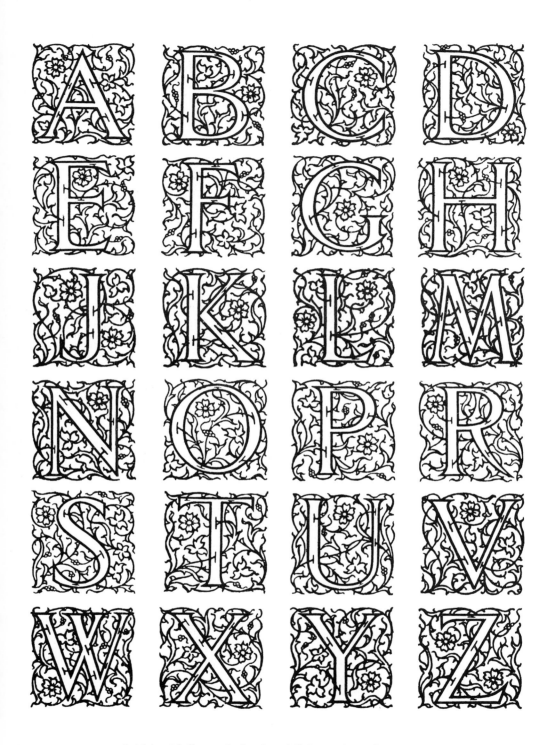

Initials with flower, leaf and tendril decorations, about 1900

So-called Walthari initials, early 20th cn.

Initial borders. Emil Rudolf Weiß, 1913

Various Art Nouveau initials

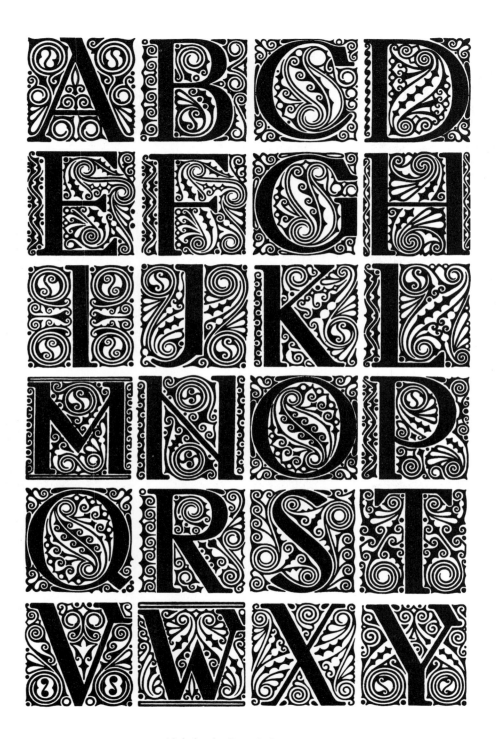

Alphabet by Peter Behrens, 1908

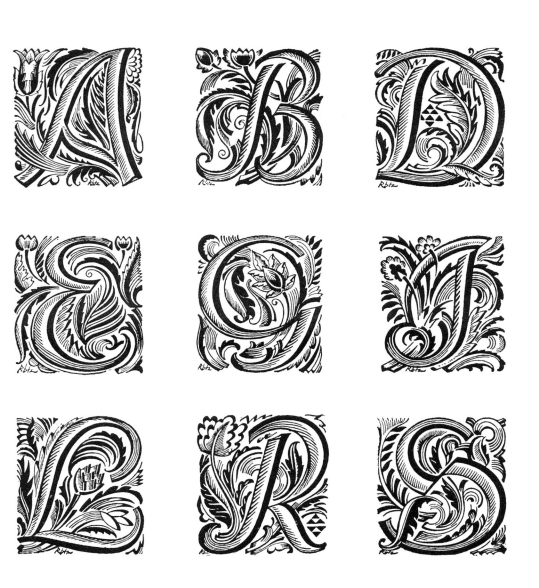

Initials by Curt Reibetanz, 1925

Appendix

Bibliography

Sources

Bauersche Gießerei, Type specimens catalogue, Frankfurt on Main, ca. 1910

Bauersche Gießerei, Werden und Wachsen einer deutschen Schriftgießerei, Frankfurt on Main 1937

1800 Woodcuts by Thomas Bewick and his school, Dover Publications, New York 1962

A. F. Butsch, Die Bücherornamentik der Renaissance, Hirth, Leipzig 1878

Max Caflisch, Kleines Spiel mit Ornamenten, Vierter Angelus-Druck, Bern 1965

Specimens of Types & Borders, H. W. Caslon & Co., London 1911

Albrecht Dürer 1471–1528, Das gesamte graphische Werk, Büchergilde Gutenberg, Frankfurt on Main

Fonderies de Caractères et leur matériel dans les pays-bas du XVᵉ au XIXᵉ Siècle. Collection Typographique de Joh. Enschedé en zonen à Haarlem, Erven F. Bohn, Haarlem 1908

Vincent Figgins, Type Specimens 1801 and 1815, Printing Historical Society, London

Martin Gerlach, Das alte Buch und seine Ausstattung vom 15. bis zum 19. Jahrhundert, Die Quelle, portfolio 13

Clarence P. Hornung (Ed.), Handbook of early Advertising Art, Dover Publications, New York 1947

Peter Jessen, Der Ornamentstich, Verlag für Kunstwissenschaft GmbH, Berlin 1920

»Monotype« Ornaments, Frederic Warde, Lanston Monotype, London 1928

Stanley Morison, The fleuron No. V, The University press, Cambridge 1926

Heinrich Olligs (Ed.), Tapeten. Ihre Geschichte bis zur Gegenwart, 3 volumes, Brunswick 1969/1970

Polytypen der Holzschnitte, W. Pfnor, Darmstadt 1839

Jan Poortenaar, Boekkunst en Grafiek, De Sikkel, Antwerp

Types and printing specimens from Matthäus Pössenbacher, bookprinters, Munich (1839)

Randeinfassungen, Initialen und Zierleisten für den Buchdruck, Reichsdruckerei Berlin 1884

John Ryder, A suite of fleurons, Phoenix House Ltd., London 1956

Schweizer Stempelschneider und Schriftgießer, adapted by Albert Bruckner on behalf of Haassche Schriftgießerei AG, Münchenstein 1943

Oliver Simon, The fleuron No. I, Office of the fleuron, London 1923

Oliver Simon, The fleuron No. IV, Office of the fleuron, London 1925

Schwarze Kunst und Weiße Kunst, type brochure of Stempel AG, Frankfurt on Main

Printing Types, Stephenson, Blake & Co. Ltd. 1924

Johann Thomas Trattner, Abdruck von Röslein und Zierrath, Vienna 1760

Das große Vignettenbuch. Bauersche Gießerei, Frankfurt on Main and Barcelona 1979

C. E. Weber, Schriftgießerei Stuttgart, taken from Lettern-Service Ingolstadt

E. R. Weiss zum fünfzigsten Geburtstage, 12. Oktober 1925. Donator Bauersche Gießerei, Frankfurt on Main

Michael Weisser, Ornament und Illustration um 1900, Fricke, Frankfurt on Main 1980

Staatliche Kunstbibliothek Berlin, Staatliche Museen Preußischer Kulturbesitz, Berlin (West): p. 299, 300, 301

Deutsches Tapetenmuseum, Kassel: p. 295, 296, 326, 327, 330

Selected literature recommended

Helmuth Theodor Bossert, Das Ornamentwerk, Ernst Wasmuth, Berlin 1937

Richard Hamann, Deutsches Ornament, Verlag des kunstgeschichtlichen Seminars der Universität Marburg, Marburg 1924

Klaus Hoffmann, Neue Ornamentik, DuMont, Cologne 1970

Claude Humbert, Ornamente, Georg D. W. Callwey, Munich

Walter Koschatzky, Die Kunst der Graphik, dtv, Munich 1975

Der große Meyers, 1906/07

Péquègnot-Schwarze, Ornamente im Laufe der Jahrhunderte, Dr. Wolfgang Schwarze, Wuppertal 1976

Heinrich Widmann, Deutsche Ornamentfibel, Staackmann, Munich 1977

Index of designers and printers